WALK LIKE AN ATHLETE

MAXIMIZING YOUR WALKING WORKOUT

By
Jeff Salvage
&
Gary Westerfield

Salvage Writes Publications
Marlton, NJ

Cover Art by:
Media Crash, Inc.
email at: *fevercat@i-2000.com*

First Printing 1996

10 9 8 7 6 5 4 3 2 1

ISBN 0-9655328-0-1
Salvage Writes Publications
86 Five Crown Royal
Marlton, NJ 08053

Printed in the U.S.A.

FOREWORD

Walking is basic to human nature. In early childhood, a baby's first steps are the pinnacle of development. Late in life, maintaining independence is equated with the ability to walk. In the years between, for most people it is the only true form of physical exercise in an average day. From a medical perspective, one of the miracles of our biology is our ability to propel ourselves in an upright posture. Indeed walking on two feet, as our primary means of ambulating, distinguishes us from other animals.

Walking in humans is a wonderfully efficient means of getting from place to place. The proper coordination of our nerves, bones, muscles, and balance system allows for smooth movements with minimal energy expenditure. Indeed, for the cost of 100 calories, a few bites of a candy bar, we can walk a mile. However, if you are trying to lose weight, a modest increase in the distance or speed of your ambulation, will, over time, burn additional calories and allow for weight loss and improved fitness.

Walking is the most natural form of exercise. It is a low-impact activity that exerts minimal stress on the joints, but still provides weight bearing that keeps the bones strong even late in life. Because we already know how to walk, and because of the low injury potential, I often suggest to my patients that they make walking their primary regular form of exercise. By walking a little faster and a little farther, even as part of a daily commute, we begin to improve our level of fitness. But to progress beyond the basic physical activity of pedestrian walking to intensive exercise and true sport we need guidance. *Walk Like an Athlete* provides this instruction.

Jeff Salvage and Gary Westerfield have masterfully distilled years of experience in competitive race walking into an easily accessible guide to help anyone transform their pedestrian gait into athletic walking. In addition to a step-by-step approach to athletic walking, this book completes the picture with guidance in stretching, nutrition, and injury treatment.

You already know how to walk: *Walk Like An Athlete* will take you the next step.

Edward M. Phillips, MD
Harvard Medical School, Department of Physical Medicine and Rehabilitation ;
Director, Outpatient Medical Services, Spaulding Rehabilitation Hospital, Boston, MA.

ACKNOWLEDGEMENTS

There are too many people who are responsible for the plethora of walking knowledge represented in this book to list them all, but we would each like to acknowledge the most influential people in our walking careers.

Ken Hendler, my high school track coach who instilled a training ethic and motivation that carried me through all my competitive days; Gary Westerfield, my coach throughout most of my competitive career, who coached me to walk and whose discussions on the physics and reasons behind how we walk resonate throughout this book; Troy Engle, who although he only coached me for a little over a year, taught me one of the most valuable lessons in walking: not to be neurotic about working out; coach Howard "Jake" Jacobson, a true friend who always looked after my welfare both as an athlete and a coach; finally, Tom Zdrojewski, one of my athletes who doesn't realize how much he kept me going all these years.

In the preparation of this book I would like to thank Tracey Briggs, Jack Starr, and Stephanie Kirk for painstakingly editing my poor excuse for grammar. I would also like to thank all my walkers in PHAST and Team in Training who have supported my efforts to write this book. (JS)

For 25 years, many athletes have trained under my guidance. Susan Liers, Lynn Weik, Tom Edwards, Curtis Fisher, Dan O'Connor and others have set American records or won national titles. Working with them and other members of the national team not only perfected my ability to coach and has been my claim to fame, but also has been very satisfying. Being in the demanding relationship as a coach to an elite walker prompted me to become more of a student of athletics than I would have as a former competitive athlete. My wife, Nadya Dimitrov, DPM, has offered immeasurable biomechanical guidance and support. Most of our walking workouts have ended up in technique discussions. My first coach, Howard "Jake" Jacobson, continues to be a sounding board for ideas. My masters walkers, Walter Hawrys, Jim McGrath, and Elton Richardson, and the constant stream of high school walkers I continue to work with, have been the motivation to perfect my presentation of athletic walking. (GW)

We would both like to thank Nadya Dimitrov, DPM for her help and guidance in writing the injury section of *Walk Like an Athlete*.

DEDICATION

This book is dedicated to my dad. Throughout the years he may not have understood my devotion to this wacky sport, but he supported me anyway. I will never forget my dad taking me to a race the day after his foot surgery - he had to stand the whole time! Unfortunately for him, the race was not a sprint, but a 26-mile marathon and it was more than two hours from our house! (JS)

This book is dedicated to the many people who asked me to talk about walking. Unknowingly, they directed me to study before I spoke. (GW)

SPECIAL THANKS

A special thanks to all those who bought advanced limited editions of *Walk Like an Athlete*. These donations helped finance this book. Without them, *Walk Like an Athlete* may never have been printed.

Color Editions

Ellen Druckenmiller	David & Carla Matusow
Eileen Druckenmiller	Linda & Sandy Fischer
Stephanie Kirk	Nadya Dimitrov
Frank Lewis	Walter Hawrys
John Albert	Erin Ward

Black & White Editions

Michelle Wink	Eileen Druckenmiller
Sharon Butler	Bill & Phyllis Hubney
Ellen Marshall	Mark Mazpink
Jack & Cathy Desomes	Bill Flick
Tom Zdrojewski	Bridget Horgan
Jack Starr	Rebecca Piorko
Stephanie Kirk	Carol Pohlig
Ellen Druckenmiller	Ed Gawinski
Ken Giannotti	Bob Davis
Cheryl Herman	Lori Ferris
George Braceland	Josh Ginsburg

TABLE OF CONTENTS

INTRODUCTION

Walk Like an Athlete has been written for people who want to learn how they can improve their walking exercise program, but not necessarily to compete. However, because the techniques explained are in most cases the same ones utilized by elite race walkers, competitors can gain much from reading *Walk Like an Athlete*. Additionally, recreational walkers can use this book to enhance their existing exercise programs. By treating the techniques introduced as a smorgasbord, they can pick only the ones they feel comfortable with trying.

Our approach in writing this book is a reflection of more than 40 years of our involvement with athletic walking. We both have competed in walking on the international level and have coached aspiring athletes to do the same. We have organized competitive race walking clubs that have attracted a diverse membership. Many of the people we have worked with have not had the dream of qualifying for the Olympics, but they have had the same desire for knowledge and expertise to guide their walking training programs. These programs are based on the athletic walking model and are designed for people who do not want to believe age is a limiting factor.

Unfortunately, due to the relative obscurity of the sport of race walking and a lack of knowledge of how athletic walking can benefit the recreational fitness enthusiast, very few qualified walking coaches exist who train their charges to be athletes. Those who do coach athletically do so primarily as coaches of elite walkers or walkers with the potential to be elite. Our background began on the same track (no pun intended), and our walking careers started with the goal of being elite race walkers. When we organized our own clubs, we offered our coaching expertise to all interested walkers. Often we have been approached to share our coaching expertise to beginning exercise walkers as well as the more serious competitors. In both cases, how we teach walking is the same; we teach it athletically. This book will show you how to **walk like an athlete**.

If you are interested in fitness, why should you *Walk Like an Athlete*?

Most people assume that walking, which appears easy, does not produce the same benefits as more traditional workouts like running, biking, or swimming. However, by walking like an athlete you can receive the benefits of these more vigorous exercises without the stress, expense, or inconvenience.

1

Athletic walking:

- is more dynamic than pedestrian walking and slow running.
- involves major body movements, working your arms, legs, and hips.
- offers greater health benefits than most people realize.

The *New England Journal of Medicine* reported in 1986 that life is extended one hour for every hour of moderate exercise. However, walking doesn't just extend your life, it also improves the quality of your life. If you walk athletically, vs. traditional pedestrian-style walking, you can:

- lose weight, because walking athletically consumes more calories and fat than traditional pedestrian walking.
- improve your cardiovascular conditioning through increased circulation.
- improve muscle tone.
- increase your range of motion through improved flexibility.
- increase agility as you age.

Walking like an athlete is the most sensible way to exercise. Athletic walking is easy to start. Unlike other activities, you don't require special equipment or places to walk. Sturdy athletic shoes, loose-fitting clothing and a desire to get fit are all you need. Athletic walking is a low intensity exercise. By working out without raising your pulse too high, you will burn more fat than runners who work at higher intensity levels. Instead, these runners tend to burn more carbohydrates, thereby reducing the amount of fat loss.

Beginning walkers will not raise their pulse to stressful levels, therefore they will not get "wiped out" with their first workout. Often when starting an exercise program, you exercise too much, get sore, and then feel discouraged from continuing.

Instead of starting a new activity, athletic walkers start with an activity with which they already are comfortable. Then, by practicing the techniques in this book, they learn how to enhance it.

Athletic walking emphasizes a relaxed and upright body posture resulting in a more efficient gait. With this technique, your skeleton supports your body, using the spine and leg bones to keep you walking tall. Compared with the hunched over technique used by runners, athletic walkers put less stress on their lower backs. Unlike runners and joggers, athletic walkers stretch their postural muscles. Athletic walkers fully extend the muscles at the back of the leg, stretching them with each stride. All of these techniques help the athletic walker combat the *middle age sag*. The tummy, posterior and thighs all get a toning workout. Keeping your posture upright can also result in better breathing, allowing your diaphragm to pull oxygen into the lungs. Walkers benefit not only from the calories burned during exercise, but from their raised metabolism which continues to expend calories throughout the day. Importantly, athletic walking technique improves blood circulation. While walking, the calf muscles contract like a "second heart," forcing blood to return to the heart. Finally, athletic walking has a calming effect on the mind. The ancient Greeks believed that walking made their minds more lucid, helping them crack problems of logic and philosophy.

All of these benefits occur while keeping impact to a minimum. While walking, the body is always in contact with the ground. This reduces the jarring motion present in running. In athletic walking, the forces produced from the body's impact with the ground are only approximately 1.25 to 1.5 times the walker's body weight. In contrast, runners strike the ground with forces three or more times the body's weight.

You may think that it's desirable to remove all impact stress; however, low impact exercise stimulates calcium deposition in the bones, retarding bone loss caused by osteoporosis. This is why non-impact sports, such as swimming, cannot meet a person's complete exercise needs.

BEFORE YOU START A WALKING PROGRAM

WHY START AN EXERCISE PROGRAM?

Many of us turn to and, unfortunately, away from exercise for diverse reasons throughout life. While people take up walking for a wide variety of reasons, there are few reasons to leave the sport. Unlike football or hockey, walking is truly a sport for life.

Our personal reasons for starting walking may not be the same as yours, but throughout the years we have coached people with almost every imaginable reason to start a regular walking program. Some are to:

- lose weight
- start a formal exercise program
- replace a sport that caused an injury
- join a group of exercise-minded people
- race walk competitively

Pick Your Own Goals!

Notice that the majority of these reasons are not based on the desire to compete. For that reason, this book does not center itself on the elite race walkers driven by a single goal of how to make the Olympic Team. Instead, it centers on making athletic walking a part of your life, allowing walking to fulfill your exercise needs. Since the reasons you may exercise vary from person to person, you should not allow someone else to dictate your needs. Because of team competition or to stroke his own ego, a coach may drive you to compete. However, if you are not competitively minded, the competition may scare you away from the other benefits of walking. To reinforce our non-competitive view, we will use the term **athletic walking**, rather than the competitive term "race walking." Being an athlete is a state of mind. It engenders the concept of a fitness-oriented role model, which attempts to maximize the benefits of an exercise program. It does **not** mean you have to compete.

A few years ago, a walker who worked out with the author for a while came regularly to practice and improved considerably. Soon she started to compete and entered the Penn Relays, the world's largest track and field meet. After finishing well in the race, a pattern soon developed. Her attendance at practice became sporadic. She explained that she felt compelled to compete if she was working out with us. Her goal was simply to work out, not to compete. She was relieved when she was told it was OK not to compete. Too many people are concerned with what other people think and not what they personally want.

Why should you start an athletic walking program?

Some people start walking because after they have been sedentary their whole lives, they reach middle age and their doctor warns them that they need to lose weight and exercise regularly. Some common choices are: to join a gym, which can be very inconvenient, not to mention expensive; to take up running, which can be very stressful, or to try walking.

Initially, many people do not visualize walking as a great form of exercise. If done athletically, it can be. Race walking, the competitive form of walking, has endured a similar lack of glory. Can you name even one elite American race walker? When was the last time you saw a walking competition on TV? Race walking has been dubbed "the Rodney Dangerfield of the track and field world," and it gets no respect. Even Gary Larson, author of *The Far Side*, printed a cartoon depicting the herbivores not being threatened by race walking cheetahs. Where race walking has gained respect has been in the minds of the people who have tried it and have realized its great benefits.

Many people who come from an athletic background believe that they can't achieve a "real" workout while walking. This is simply untrue. People often ask us if they can get their heart rate up while walking (We have both clocked our heart rate at more than 200 beats per minute, close to our theoretical maximum.) We usually respond by asking if the person would get his or her heart pounding running a 6-minute mile. They say sure, if they could run that fast. We then ask what they think walking a mile that fast would do. *(The world record for walking is well under six minutes a mile.)*

Even if you don't want to walk anywhere near that fast, by using the techniques used in race walking, athletic walking workouts can be as vigorous as running workouts, without the added pounding and risk of injury.

We are sure that once you have tried athletic walking you will respect it as a great form of exercise.

It's Never Too Late

Don't let age be an excuse. Many members of our clubs did not get interested in walking until they retired and were senior citizens. Faced with the golden years of their lives, these walkers were blessed with plenty of time to exercise and stretch. They could choose any sport their bodies would allow, but that's just it. Most people's bodies can't take the stress of other sports. Many people decide to take up walking as a form of exercise because they are unable to continue with whatever sport they participated in when they were younger. Barry Foster, a Pro-Bowl football player, just retired after a couple of years of professional ball. He said that he felt like a 60-year-old man when he tried to run. An exercise program should build you up, not break you down.

Walking allows people to start slowly and build gradually. The level people reach is dictated by their own time and commitment level. We have found the retired walkers in our clubs to be some of the most enjoyable to coach. They listen and have the time to do everything we tell them, and they get results. Many of the individuals we coach on a regular basis and some who we coach by mail are among the top walkers in their age groups in the country. None of these walkers walked competitively when they were younger. It's never too late to start. Make a goal to get started now, if you haven't already done so. Do it now!

Other Forms of Exercise May Not Be Enough

Some people want to walk simply to augment another training program. They may swim a couple of times a week, but that doesn't prevent osteoporosis, not to mention that we all do not have pools in our back yards. What we all do have is access to a road or park. The basic idea is: You can walk when you want, where you want, and how much you want. You need minimal equipment and do not require anyone else to do it. So just go do it!

Don't Let Time Be an Issue

Time is the single biggest reason we hear for why people do not exercise. It is also our single biggest reason for not exercising more. If you make exercise a part of your life, like brushing your teeth in the morning, it will be habitual. All our friends know what night we coach, and we walk while we coach. On the weekends our training partners come over in the early morning and we work out. These times are almost non-negotiable. If we can, we walk other days during the week, but the days we coach ensure that we maintain a minimum acceptable level of fitness. By walking every week at the same time, it becomes a part of our routine and we don't think about it.

Hidden Benefits

There are many hidden benefits to a walking or exercise program that people do not initially realize. The first is all the wonderful places that you find as you meander throughout your neighborhood. Most neighborhoods have something worth finding, you just have to look. Near our homes in New Jersey and New York, we have trees, lakes, and ponds. If you live in a city, you may have parks or perhaps old architecture populating the landscape.

The author often travels for business and works a couple of days wrapped around a weekend. Wherever he goes, he tries to visit the attractions of the region. On a business trip to Arizona, the site to see was the Grand Canyon. Unfortunately, he had but one day to play. So, he drove four hours to the canyon, hiked a couple of miles with a friend, sent him back up and went all the way down and back in a total of five hours. The walk was about 16 miles and dropped about 4,000 feet on the way down. Had the author not been in excellent walking shape, he would never have seen the incredible sights as he wound down the canyon. Upon arriving at the top, his friend was sleeping in the car. It is a shame that he does not participate in a walking program. Look what he missed.

People were standing on the top of the Grand Canyon and simply looking at the view. They thought it was breathtaking. They have no idea how much more they missed by not walking down the trail.

Like many of the bystanders who claimed they were too old to walk down the trail, many people claim they cannot train like an athlete. While we would not expect beginning athletic walkers to complete a round trip in five hours, if they have been on a regular athletic walking program, they certainly could walk it at a leisurely pace. At a minimum, they could walk at least halfway down and back and see more of nature's panorama. We are quite confident that walkers who train athletically experience more of what the world has to offer than those who do not. Being healthier improves your senses and gives you a greater appreciation for life.

FEEL THE NEED FOR SPEED

When people first think about walking, their first thoughts are not usually about speed. Either they are concerned with other goals (they want to lose weight or increase their fitness level), or they do not believe that they can walk faster. Many beginning walkers have approached us stating that they cannot walk any faster no matter what they do. By modifying their style to utilize the techniques of athletic walkers, they could break through this speed barrier.

With athletic walking technique, you will not only walk faster, but burn more calories per mile. In addition, by walking athletically you will walk faster and not have to dedicate as much time to your exercise program.

If your goal is to walk five miles, five days a week, and you are walking 15 minutes a mile, you will spend on average six and ¼ hours per week, or 325 hours a year, exercising. In contrast, if you are walking 10-minute miles you will be able to burn about the same number of calories in five hours a week, or 260 hours a year. That means you've saved 65 hours, almost **three days** a year.

Athletic Walking Is Not Just About Going Fast

To discover what other goals you might achieve by walking athletically, ask yourself, why do athletes train? Usually to go faster, which is their primary goal. But they go faster because they are either better conditioned, stronger, or more efficient. Being efficient, stronger, or more conditioned is a secondary goal. As an athletic walker, walking efficiently, while keeping stress to the body to a minimum, is the primary goal. By being efficient, you will be faster.

The style of walking that we teach to allow this increase in speed is the same style used by competitive race walkers. Please don't be scared off by that term. We will not force you to conform to a specific style. Our goal is to teach people, within their comfort level and desire, the athletic techniques used by race walkers to maximize their walking workouts.

If we surveyed any group of individuals using walking as their primary form of exercise, we would find that many people are calling their walking activity by different names: Healthwalking[1], power walking, and exercise walking are all names attributed to walking for exercise. Since there is no formal definition of these forms of walking, they may vary or overlap in definition from person to

---

[1] * Howard "Jake" Jacobson first dubbed the term healthwalking as a verb to describe walking for health back in 1981. He purposely spells it as one word to distinguish that healthwalking is an activity in and of itself.

person. From now on, we will refer to non-race walking techniques under the catch phrase **healthwalking**.

How does athletic walking differ from healthwalking? When you walk athletically, you will feel faster and more fluid in your movements. You accomplish a change from being very mechanical and deliberate in each movement to being continuous and fluid, relying upon a force generated from each previous movement (momentum). Mechanical movements can be thought of as movements in which after you complete each one, you must start over again. The stopping and starting is very inefficient. When an athletic walker or race walker masters the techniques explained in *Walk Like an Athlete*, he or she will feel a sensation that movement is continuous, that each stride flows into the next without the herky-jerky style caused by repeatedly starting and stopping each action.

Additionally, as you go faster, you will utilize more of your muscles. One coach says that race walkers utilize more than 95% of their muscles, in contrast to healthwalkers, who use about 70%. By utilizing the additional muscle groups, athletic walkers get a more balanced workout and tone some of those hard to reach areas. A result of this extra muscle work is that the more athletic race walkers burn 130 calories per mile compared with 100 calories per mile for the non-athletic healthwalkers.

Since athletic walkers are burning more calories, does this mean that athletic walkers waste more energy? Yes, but consider the fact that they are moving much faster than health walkers, and as they approach the speed of runners, their technique allows them to continue walking without switching over to running. Athletic walkers must work harder at these speeds to continue walking and to receive the benefit of less impact stress than running at the same speed.

Another benefit of increased muscle use is that you will burn more calories all day long. As you work out more of your muscles, you will be increasing the muscle mass of your body. Muscle burns more calories than fat, even when you are just sitting around the house. Therefore, by utilizing more muscle in your walking workout, you will increase your calorie burning all day.

Now that we have gotten you excited about walking athletically, one word of caution. Before you put the proverbial foot forward, you should **consult your doctor** and get approval for the program you are about to undertake. Please be sure to explain both your distance and time goals. Although this book provides guidelines and advice on many health-related issues (nutrition, injury prevention, rehabilitation from injuries, etc.), it is not a substitute for a physician's appraisal of any problems that you incur.

SOME SIMPLE ADVICE ON WALKING SHOES

When choosing your walking shoes, don't be a slave to fashion. Buy walking shoes because they are quality shoes, not because they make you look cool or color coordinated. One could think that the shoe companies purposely made their high quality shoes look ugly to see who were the serious athletes.

You should wear your walking shoes only when working out. So, if you can afford to have a separate pair from your everyday pair, it is preferable. Additionally, it is often better to have more than one pair of training shoes. Switching between two pairs will give your feet a break and help prevent blisters. Also, by having an extra pair, you do not have to worry about having to wear wet shoes when working out. You can wear the other pair while the first one is drying out.

How much should you spend on walking shoes?

Price obviously is a reflection of your budget. If you can afford it, we recommend walking shoes between $60 and $80. Those that are more expensive are usually so only because the shoe companies know that people are willing to pay more. While more expensive shoes may be marginally better, quality does not necessarily increase proportionately with price. Also, be aware that walking shoes that are really inexpensive are usually less supportive, less stable, or less comfortable.

One way to save a considerable amount of money is to buy discontinued walking shoes. Shoes get discontinued most often due to fashion. It is not uncommon for these shoes to be discounted 30% or more, and they are every bit as functional as when they were full price.

What brand is best?

Choice of a favorite brand is very subjective. Don't pick the brands that are geared toward fashion. Pick the tried and true athletic brands and make sure that you pick one that is comfortable. You should realize that everyone's feet are different, so what is comfortable for someone else may not be for you. If you have a narrow foot you may like Nikes. If your foot is a little wider, you may like the Asics or New Balance brands. If you use an orthotic[2], make sure the shoe is deep enough to accommodate it. Try the orthotic in the shoe before you buy it. Try different brands, walk around in them (in the same style that you use when you walk), in the same types of socks that you wear to walk.

---

[2] An orthotic is a custom shoe implant that is designed to help control irregular foot motion.

Should I buy a walking or running shoe?

This question depends a lot on whether or not you want to walk athletically or walk like a pedestrian. If you wish to walk athletically, it is our preference to buy running shoes and walk in them. We find the proper running shoes are more stable and durable. However, if you are walking like a pedestrian, a quality pair of walking shoes may be more comfortable. Either way, we would pick a shoe with the following characteristics:

- Low heel.
- Stable heel counter (to prevent excessive motion at heel contact). If you squeeze either side of the heel together, it should not collapse.
- Flexible toe (break across the ball of the foot or toe joints).
- Ample toe-box (Not too narrow or shallow).
- Shoe last (the design of the bottom of the shoe, whether it is straight or curved in), a consideration for people who over pronate or over supinate[3]. Because it is very difficult to tell the difference between straight- and curve-lasted shoes, we suggest you discuss this matter with both your physician and qualified shoe salesperson.
- Sturdy sole: You should not be able to bend the shoe in half. Any shoe you are considering should be able to pass a simple test. Hold the shoe by the heel and toe, flex it up from the toe. It should bend only where the ball of your foot would be in the shoe. Do not consider a shoe that bends under the arch, because it will collapse under the middle of your foot. Turn the shoe sole up and hold it in the same places. Now twist the bottom of the shoe. It should be slightly flexible; discard any shoes that are very flexible. They will not support your foot.
- Lightweight racing flats are not suited for athletic walking training.

Where should I buy my walking shoes?

Initially, we recommend going to a specialty store. Don't go to a chain store, where high school kids (no offense) are giving you advice. Until you find a walking shoe that you are happy with, get the best advice that you can. Once you've selected a pair you are comfortable with, stick with the same model. You can buy additional ones wherever you like. We often buy from catalogs. If your model of walking shoe is discontinued, that does not mean there is anything wrong with them; buy them at a reduced price. We often buy extra pairs to save money.

---

[3] Pronate and supinate are conditions where feet roll in or out excessively.

When should I buy a new pair of walking shoes?

Don't wait until your walking shoes are worn to find another pair. It is a good idea to have the next pair on hand. When you realize that you need a new pair, life often gets in the way and you tend to procrastinate. Another common problem may be that the store you go to does not have anything that is comfortable for you. Then you have placed yourself in the position of having to walk in worn out shoes. In addition, don't buy your shoes early in the morning. After walking around for the better part of a day, the shoes you purchased in the morning will feel much tighter.

When are walking shoes worn out?

As a general rule of thumb, you should replace your walking shoes when you have walked in them for about 400 miles. However, everyone is different. Some people strike harder than others, and thus wear out the outer sole and collapse the mid-sole quicker. Additionally, some walking shoes wear better than others. By looking at the bottom and sides of the walking shoes, you can tell when it is time for them to be replaced.

Walking shoes can wear out in many places. Simply waiting until there are holes in them or your feet start to hurt is not a good idea. As a walker you will tend to wear out your walking shoes at the outer heel and at the point where you push off with your big toe.

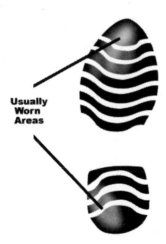

**Usually
Worn
Areas**

Also, if your walking shoes are soft or you strike the ground very hard, you may compress the heel. You may also see your walking shoe leaning to one side. If your walking shoes clearly exhibit these signs, it is time to discard them.

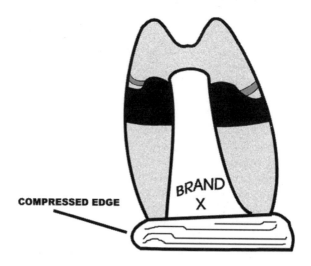

Finally, look at the condition of the upper part of the shoe, the cloth and "leather" combinations that hold the foot in place. If the stitching is coming apart or you can feel that the heel counter is broken, then it is time to replace the shoes.

Do I need to break in a new pair of walking shoes?

Most people need to break in walking shoes. This will help prevent blisters and other foot ailments. It is best to do so before your old ones wear out. First, wear them around the house. If they are comfortable, wear them for a few short workouts, progressively increasing the distance you wear them.

When should I throw out my old shoes?

This may seem like a ridiculous question, but it is not. Most people will throw out their shoes when they are worn out or when they get a new pair. If you do, you are throwing out an excellent source of knowledge about how you walk. If you do get an injury, your doctor may ask you to bring an old pair of shoes with you. By observing the wear pattern of the shoes, the doctor may be better able to diagnose your problem.

LAST TIDBITS BEFORE STARTING DOWN THE TRAIL

How much should I drink when I walk?

Plenty, especially during hot and humid weather. By the time you feel thirsty, it is already too late.

It is important to drink before, during, and after your walking workout. It is not enough to drink only while working out. We try to drink water or a sports drink that replaces electrolytes[4] and carbohydrates (either works fine, it is a matter of personal preference) periodically during the day, especially in the summertime.

When going on a long walk, be prepared. Some walking areas may not have water readily accessible; carry a bottle in a "fanny pack" or hide bottles of water on your walking course before you begin.

A method used by many athletes to determine how dehydrated they are after a workout is to observe the color of their urine. Crystal clear usually means that you have taken in enough water, while stark yellow can mean that you are not drinking enough. (Be careful, stark yellow urine may also be a sign that you are taking more vitamins than your body is absorbing.)

What and when can one eat before walking?

Later in this book are more details about nutrition, but for now, follow a sensible diet. A little moderation can go a long way. By balancing the amount of carbohydrates, proteins, and fats in your diet you can feel great and walk well.

Too many people are on a *"remove all fat from the diet"* kick. While Americans generally eat too much fat, too little fat is not healthy, either. Your body needs a certain amount of fat to operate properly. Simply replacing fat with sugar substitutes is not going to solve all your nutritional needs.

For now, our advice is to eat lots of complex carbohydrates. Try to eat fruits and vegetables every day, and if you want a cookie, have a cookie. Just don't have the whole bag. Occasional small snacks aren't going to destroy a diet and may allow you to continue with your diet program longer.

Because every person is different, we can all tolerate different things in our diet and exercise program. It is very difficult to give generic advice about what and

---

[4] Electrolytes are the salts and minerals the body loses while working out.

when a person can eat before working out. Some people have a hardy stomach and can eat within an hour of working out. In fact, some people need to eat something in the morning before they work out or their stomach gets aggravated. The best solution is to experiment and record what works for you. Do not try to mimic the elite athletes or your friends, because their needs may differ from yours.

Similarly, on long walks some people like to eat something, while others do not. Personally, the author likes to eat a banana or one of the nutritional sports bars, but some individuals have difficulty digesting these. Again, try them out and see what is best for you.

What items should I be aware of when I walk?

This may be one of the most important pieces of advice we can give you. When participating in a walking program, always record your walking progress in a training log. Besides enabling you to chart your progress, a training log is an excellent tool for injury prevention and diagnosis.

When you train, you should record your mileage, pace, general feeling about effort and any extenuating circumstances. This can include:

- Soreness or acute injury
- Extreme weather conditions
- Lack of sleep
- Stress at the workplace

It is also a good idea to record your resting pulse rate when you wake up in the morning. If your pulse is higher than normal, take it easy. You might need a rest, you may have done too much or you may be catching a "bug."

If you are developing or have a problem, you should consult a doctor or coach. By having your training log on hand, you can go over what led up to your problem and help prevent it from occurring in the future.

Some simple advice

We follow a simple philosophy, and it is **not** "No Pain, No Gain." We believe in the **Minimum Effort, Maximum Gain** philosophy. By using all resources at your disposal, you should attempt to reduce the effort it takes to get the maximum benefit from your exercise program.

HISTORY

While we can go into a long history on competitive walking, that would be boring. Instead, the tale of Guiseppi Walker will do just fine.

Many assume that race walking is a relatively new sport, but it really has been around for quite some time. Race walking's origins are traced to a small Italian town, in the mid 1800s, where a poor old shoemaker named Guiseppi Walker lived.

Unlike most of the shoemakers of the 19th century, "Joe" was not happy with his position in the caste system. He aspired to greatness. He worked hard to make the best shoes available. As one of the first documented cases of *guerrilla marketing*, he demonstrated the effectiveness of his shoes by betting that he could outdistance anyone in the town.

Although most people generally chalked the old man's antics up to the eccentricity of an aging craftsman, he was able to eke out a living from his trade. All this would change upon his son, Joe Walker Jr., reaching manhood.

Joe Walker Jr., like many children, rebelled. Instead of following in his dad's footsteps, no pun intended, he took up drinking and frolicking.

Joe Walker Jr., also competed, but not to see how far he could walk. Instead, he followed the age-old tradition of *walking* the town. His walk consisted of having a drink in every bar in town. The town the Walkers lived in actually had competitions to see how quickly one could complete the "course."

Although Joe Jr. was quite the drinker, he lost the competition year after year to leaner, more athletic men. So, begrudgingly, he asked his dad for help. Although, Joe Jr.'s goal was not a lofty one, Guiseppi was glad to see his son finally committed to something and crafted his best shoes to date. To further improve performance, he taught his son to push off more with his feet, to swing his hips, and use his arms to counter balance his stride. After a few short lessons, Joe Jr. was walking with what has come to be thought of as traditional race walking style.

Joe Jr., embarrassed by the unusual style of walking, would lace up and train only at night. Later, his shoes would be dubbed *sneakers*, and the athletic shoe industry was born.

Joe Jr. trained well and was soon able to beat the entire town. Over time, the sport outgrew its alcohol-laden roots (with a short relapse in the early 1980s at the U.S. Olympic Training Center) and graduated into a serious track and field event.

If you believe this whimsical story, we have some wonderful swampland down in Florida to sell you.

The Real History

Even though race walking has been a men's event in the Olympics since 1908, and one of the distances contested is currently the longest foot race in the games (31 miles), it is often considered the Rodney Dangerfield event of athletics.

The sport of walking has gone through an evolution. If we are a little liberal with our definition of walking, we can find its roots traced back to as early as 2,500 BC, where Egyptian hieroglyphics recorded the first written record of a walking competition. However, what actually differentiated walking from running in these early competitions? In the early Greek civilization, there was no distinction made between running and walking.

It was not until the early 14th century that a formal definition of the sport could be found in France. However, much of walking's early publicity centered around bets and other financial rewards. In 1589, an English nobleman bet he could walk non-stop for 300 miles. This is a far cry from the 5K weekend shuffles that we are accustomed to, but these early walks were the beginnings of regularly held walking events. By the 1800s, walking entered its "Golden Era," where walking competitions were seen regularly in fairs and festivals; however it was not until 1837 that **race walking** was listed as a formal sport.

One of the more famous American forefathers of athletic walking was Edward Weston, a walker from the Civil War era. During this time, many walking competitions were professional. Either prize money or bets provided opportunity for individuals to make large sums of money for their walking excursions. In fact, Edward Weston made more money in one race than the salary of a professional baseball player in his day.

Why did Weston take up walking astronomical distances in the mid 1800s? Simple: he lost a bet. Weston's first major walk occurred because he bet that President Lincoln would lose the 1860 election. The restitution from the bet was that he had to walk from Boston to the inauguration in Washington, D.C. While Edward Weston is credited as being one of America's race walking forefathers, he was not necessarily using the same race walking gait that we use today.

18

Many of the competitions in the 1800s did not adhere to the strict race walking style used in competition today. Instead, race walking started out as more of a "Go As You Please" event. This meant that people walked a little and then ran a little. Quite a contrast from today's race walks in which judges are always keeping a watchful eye on the competitors.

We believe that the reason race walking has not received the notoriety of other track and field events is that the United States performs below the standards we achieve in most other track and field events. We have never won an Olympic gold medal. The United States has won the bronze medal only twice. Many forget that it was not until Frank Shorter won the Olympic marathon that the running boom started in America.

While many people believe running is more popular than race walking, how many people really run? Most runners are actually joggers. However, we know there are an estimated 80 million people in this country who walk regularly as a form of exercise. This is many more than the number of runners and joggers combined. Since race walking is the competitive form of healthwalking, we can say that race walking and healthwalking are actually more popular than running.

DEFINITION

When one of the authors was younger, he felt first-hand the differences between running and race walking. He worked at a restaurant that had an annual fishing trip. The first year he went, he strapped on his backpack and jogged about five miles to the boat. The backpack bounced up and down, but he didn't think much about it. The next year, he strapped the same backpack on his shoulders, but instead of running, he race walked to the boat. Instead of bouncing up and down, the backpack swung from side to side. The change in motion of the backpack was an indication of the change in his locomotive style. It also was an indication that he had changed from a pounding form of exercise to a form that sent the stress from side to side.

By definition, race walking does not vary much from the type of walking we are currently calling healthwalking. However, race walkers do many things that increase their pace, aerobic benefit, and muscle use over the typical health walkers. You may take advantage of the benefits of race walking techniques by picking up as many of the following guidelines as you desire. In competition however, you must obey the rules below.

Race walking's two rules are:

- **Race Walking is a progression of steps so taken that the walker makes contact with the ground so that no visible (to the human eye) loss of contact occurs.** This means that before you lift your rear foot off the ground, the leading foot must make contact with the ground. As a healthwalker, the odds are that you are already obeying this rule. Only faster walkers and runners have problems with this rule. This rule has an added benefit. The requirement of maintaining constant contact with the ground reduces the pounding on your body and helps prevent injuries.

- The second rule is the one that most people have an initial problem grasping. **The advancing leg must be straightened (i.e., not bent at the knee) from the moment of first contact with the ground until in the vertical position.** When beginning walkers first hear this rule they sometimes think that they must walk with their legs straight all the time. This is incorrect. If you tried to walk with straight legs all the time, you would look like the Frankenstein monster. The only stipulation to obey this rule is that when your forward foot strikes the ground, your leg should be straight. It must stay straight until it passes under the body. Then you will have to bend it to swing it forward.

LEARNING TO WALK

To walk like an athlete, practice and perfect your technique before trying to go too fast. If you practice walking with the wrong technique, your early mistakes will be difficult to correct.

The more athletic walking techniques you master, whether you race walk or healthwalk, the more you use your body's previously untapped resources, increasing your pace and improving the safety of your walking workout.

Remember, it is difficult to pick up any new skill. Take your time. Techniques are learned over weeks; they cannot be learned all at once. We will present our techniques in steps so that you build fitness as you master the athletic walking style.

When the author teaches people at his walking clinics, he breaks down the techniques. He teaches one section a night and allows the individual to practice these techniques during the week. As the new walkers practice these techniques, they build the muscles required to walk correctly. The next week, all the techniques are reviewed, and if the person has mastered them, he moves on to the next session. If not, he continues to review and practice the techniques for another week. Do not get frustrated if you do not master every technique. Some techniques will come easier than others and even elite walkers work constantly to improve their form.

Do as I Say

Be careful to respond to what is said. Do not mimic what people do. By looking at and copying someone you think has excellent form, you may be misleading yourself. Most people have something unique about their body structure that affects the way they walk. This is commonly referred to as someone's "style." Style varies from technique, because although we all strive to walk with the same mechanics, we all have different bodies. While it would be convenient for every body part to be in exactly the "correct" proportion with the rest of the body, the fact is that many of us have body parts that are larger or shorter than average. Some people have long legs and a short torso, others have forearms that are disproportionally large. These variances will cause a person to walk slightly differently than what would be considered textbook technique, but that is **your** style. By trying to mimic someone else's style, you may be learning a bad habit or one that you are not ready to learn. Also, someone you may be watching may walk with an efficient style, but it may lead to more injuries. This book's main objective is to teach safe techniques.

Too much, too soon

When you first practice the athletic walking technique, mix the new technique with your original pedestrian or healthwalking style. This will prevent overuse of untrained muscles.

When trying a new technique, pick a distance, such as the distance between two telephone poles. Walk this distance with the athletic walking technique and then walk the distance between the next two telephone poles with your pedestrian, or healthwalking, style. Repeat this technique throughout your walk. If the distance between two telephone poles is too short, try the distance between three or four poles. If the distance between two poles is too long, try half that distance. What, you don't have any poles in your neighborhood? Use a few houses or stores. For urban walkers, use a city block.

The important thing is to listen to your body. If something aches constantly while you are walking, you are walking too much with the new technique. Do not overdo it. You are learning a style of walking that will benefit you for your whole life. Rushing to learn everything in one week will not have a profound effect on your lifetime health. It may, however, cause you to get sore and frustrated to the point where you quit. That will have a profound effect on your long-term health.

This is not a college sport in which you have only four years to participate. So relax and take your time learning the technique. On the flip side, you do need to push yourself a little. If you never exert yourself to walk athletically, you may never feel its speed and dynamic gracefulness. A balance must be kept.

Don't obsess on numbers

In the beginning, don't pay attention to numbers. Too much stress is placed on trying to walk an exact time or attain an exact pulse range. How many of you have been frustrated trying to count your pulse after a workout, only to get an inaccurate reading? Instead, measure your exertion by how you feel. By learning to gauge your exertion level you will be more relaxed and enjoy the workout more.

No weights, please

Often the first question asked by beginning walkers is, "Can I use hand and ankle weights when I walk?" Do not walk with weights on your legs or in your hands. They will add stress to the body in a way that it was not designed to handle. Athletic walking gives your body a significant workout and eliminates the perceived need for weights.

It is much better to learn proper technique, so you can walk faster and get a better workout, than to increase your exertion by using weights. While walking with weights does require more effort than walking at the same pace without them, it also raises your risk of injuries to unacceptable levels. Walking with weights also throws off your cadence, making proper technique difficult, if not impossible.

BASIC ATHLETIC WALKING TECHNIQUE

Before you learn to walk faster, you must learn to walk efficiently and safely. This may require you to slow your pace for a short time. However, this allows you to build solid skills allowing you to walk faster later.

Foot placement

Walk on a straight line?

Imagine there is a thin, straight line extending in front of you and down the path that you are walking. (If you go to a track, use one of the lane lines.) When walking at a pedestrian pace, without using any of the athletic walking techniques, each foot should land just on either side of the line.

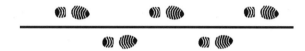

As your pace quickens a little bit, your feet will land just on the edge of that line.

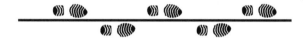

If you watch race walkers or fully trained athletic walkers, you will see that their feet will approach landing in almost an exact straight line. When you learn how to use your hips efficiently, your foot placement will change slightly to imitate this near straight line placement. Be aware, if you try to mimic this action without using your hips, you will place an unneeded stress across your knee.

Never allow your feet to cross over the line as depicted in the following figure.

Foot strike

When your foot strikes the ground, land on the back of your heel and point your toes as high as you can.

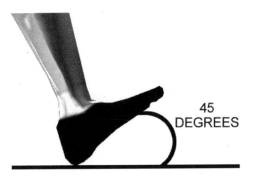

Once your foot has made contact, roll it forward, keeping the toes off the ground until your leg is supporting your body's weight. How long the toes are kept off the ground is directly related to the strength of your shin. When you walk with your toes pointed, you will be using your shin muscle more. As you learn this technique, it may cause a burning sensation in your shins. When you feel this soreness, back off a little and then try the new technique again. Your goal will eventually be to hold your foot at a 45-degree angle with the ground at heel strike. Avoid slapping your foot against the ground. Instead, roll onto the mid-part of your foot and finally through your big toe.

Some people's foot placement will naturally point out or in because of the way they are built. If that's you, do not try to change your foot placement when you walk athletically. By using your hips properly, your foot falls will occur in a straight line, but the feet will not be parallel. While this is less efficient, forcing you to straighten your foot placement may cause unnecessary stress on your legs, feet, and knees. The following figures show the foot placement of a walker who is landing with his toe pointed in (upper figure) and with his toe pointed out (lower figure).

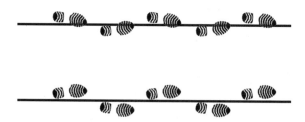

Transition from one leg to the other

We mentioned earlier that an athletic walker should have a smooth, non-mechanical motion. The transition from one leg to the other leg is the key to a smooth motion. A visualization that helps is to think of an athletic walker's leg transition as similar to a log rolling along. There is no beginning or ending to a log's rolling motion. Similarly, your leg motion should be one continuous motion without a start and stop. You should not feel like a car with a square wheel, thumping against the ground from step to step.

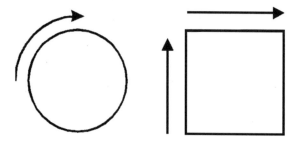

Sometimes, awkwardness is caused by the way you place your feet on the ground. If your shins are weak, you may land with a pointed toe, only to have your foot flatten quickly. If this happens to you, make sure you do the shin exercises and stretches explained later on regular basis.

If you are walking efficiently, the transition flows from one leg to another without any jerky movements. Remember, the goal is to help the body go forward, so any excess motion that you get from shifting your weight side to side is undesirable.

STRAIGHTENING YOUR LEG

If you are serious about trying to walk athletically, you **must** pay attention to this technique. At the beginning, adding this action may slow you down, but there is a return on the investment. Even if you do not wish to compete, there are some health benefits to this technique as well.

After you master pointing your toe on placement and rolling off the toe, try to straighten your knee when your heel strikes the ground. The rules of race walking state that you must straighten your knee on contact, and it must stay straight until your body passes over the leg. Efficient athletic walking makes use of the same straight leg technique. A straight leg, upon heel contact, allows you to gain more leverage than landing on a bent leg, and you don't have to waste energy pulling the knee back. (Of course, remember that as your leg swings forward, you must bend it.)

It is helpful to visualize your lower leg being attached to your upper leg by a hinge. As you swing your upper leg forward, your lower leg should swing forward as well, straightening as your heel strikes the ground.

The final benefit of landing with a straight knee is to lessen the stress to the knee. With proper technique, the thighs and hips absorb the force of landing rather than the knees. While you may worry that your hips might start to hurt, this usually isn't the case. The hip is a larger, less abused joint and can generally handle more stress than your knee.

ADD POWER TO YOUR STRIDE

HIP MOTION

While using your legs efficiently is important, the movement of the hips is the primary source of forward locomotion provided by the body. Your hips are positioned at the top of your legs. By rotating the hips forward, the swinging leg is pulled off the ground. By pivoting the hips from one leg to the other and driving the swinging leg forward, the hips act like a motor, propelling the body forward one step at a time.

If this description is a little confusing, it is simpler to try the following exercise than to try to understand a detailed written description of the hip motion.

1. Find a fairly long, steep hill. At the base, start walking as quickly as you can, except hold your arms across your chest, much like a vampire in a coffin. This will prevent your arms from counter balancing the forces in your hips.

2. For about 15 yards, walk uphill as quickly as you can. You will feel a tugging sensation in your hips. Continue walking, but for the next 15 yards try to exaggerate the sensation you are feeling in your hips. Allow your muscles to work with your hips to follow the motion of the tugs. This motion should be forward and back, not side to side.

3. Finally, bring your arms down into normal walking position. Allow them to swing, and continue to exaggerate your hips as you have been doing. Your hip and swing leg will feel as if they are being whipped forward as you swing your arm back.

You should notice a dramatic effect. Your stride should feel more powerful and longer.

Try this exercise a couple of times. Now try to walk with your improved style on flat ground. Finally, repeat the exercise on flat ground.

If during the course of your workout, you feel like you are slowing down and are no longer using your hips properly, repeat the exercise. Even without the hill, it can be a good refresher.

If this exercise does not work, or if there is no hill in your neighborhood, you might try an analogy. Think of yourself as a gunslinger. Imagine you have two pistols holstered on your hips. Imagine walking through saloon doors and pushing them open with the guns on your hips, one at a time. As you imagine the door swinging back, also imagine that your hips guided the guns to push the doors. Now try to walk with the sensation that you feel in your hips as you attempted to push the doors in both directions.

Benefits

Increased stride length

Compared with normal pedestrian and health walking, athletic walking's proper hip action naturally lengthens the stride at the top of the legs. Do not try to reach out too far in front of your body; you don't have to. By using your hips properly, you will increase your stride length without overstriding. Having too long of a stride will slow you down.

By pivoting your hip forward, as in the right figure, you can increase stride length on average of six inches. Also notice that by rotating your hip forward, your foot placement is now closer to a straight line. When your hips are not utilized, your legs' effective range of motion is limited.

Reducing the braking force

All coaches agree that overstriding slows you down. But what is the definition of overstriding? A simple definition is:

> Overstriding is when a walker takes too long a stride, either in front or behind the body, such that the extra stride length actually slows the forward progress of the walker.

We are not overstriding when we increase the stride length using the hips, because by rotating our hips we are not changing the angle the forward leg makes with the ground. Taking a long stride in front of your body without the proper hip placement causes your leading foot to strike the ground at an angle that allows a force to occur from the ground that pushes you back. We refer to this force as the **braking force**. By driving your hips forward and backward, we can reduce the angle our leg makes with the ground. This will reduce the braking force the ground exerts on your body.

Increased speed

The hips, directing the forward leg movement and the body's forward progress, can be used to increase leg speed. While you want to continue to utilize the methods we mentioned with regard to your legs, visualize your hips (or the six guns at the front of your thighs) leading your legs and feet. Increasing the speed of your hips will directly increase the speed of your legs.

ARMS

The use of the arms is one of the most controversial and misunderstood actions in competitive walking. Pumping your arms high and hard is not the way to a quick efficient stride. Contrary to popular belief, your arms can move only as fast as your hips and legs. Since mechanically the arms only serve to counterbalance leg movements, simply moving your arms faster will not increase the speed of your stride, and it will throw off your body's natural timing.

Instead of pumping them, think of your arms mimicking the actions of a pendulum of a clock. On each stroke, a pendulum swings back and forth with minimal effort. Due to the pendulum's lack of resistance, it requires little effort to keep it moving. What effort is required is generated from a small motor located at the top of the pendulum. Your arms are attached in a similar fashion at the shoulders. To keep your arms moving, you need to "motor" them from the shoulder. However, you do not have to pump them vigorously. By relaxing your shoulders, and pulling your arms backward in a motion that counter balances your forward moving hip and swinging leg, you accomplish the necessary arm motion with the least amount of effort.

How do you know if your arms and hips are synchronized? Try this simple drill. While walking like an athlete, drop your hands to your side with your palms facing back. As you walk forward, allow your arms to swing. Feel the forward thrusting movement of your hips. During long walks you may want to try this to "reconnect" with your hips.

Relaxed shoulders

Relaxing your shoulders can be difficult. Many people believe they have relaxed their shoulders, but they are still carrying their shoulders higher than they should. When walking, your shoulders often tighten and have a tendency to rise above the desired position. By observing the height of your shoulders, you can check to see if they are relaxed. Since you won't be carrying a ruler while you walk, simply place one hand on your shoulder and lower it as far down as it can go. When your shoulder is all the way down, it is in the relaxed position.

Arm angle

A common misconception is that you should hold your arms at a 90 degree angle. For some people, this may be correct, but it is not the ideal for all. The ideal arm swing is for your hand to travel from a couple of inches behind your hip to the chest line. But how do you accomplish the proper range of motion for your arm swing?

If you hold your arms at a 90-degree angle, you might have difficulty maintaining an arm swing in the correct range of motion. You may have to hold your arms at a different angle from someone else, because the ratio of the length of each part of the arm to the other may vary from person to person. If your arms are swinging too far in front of the body, you will have to pull your arm back excessively to keep it in the proper range of motion. This braking action that you add to your arm swing is a waste of energy. Similarly, if your arms are not swinging forward enough, you are forced to add an accelerating action. A similar action would be required if your arm was too far behind the hip or not far enough behind the hip. Any of these efforts would be wasted energy.

Instead of trying to control your arm swing by effort, try modifying the angle of the arm. This will allow you to easily control the destination of the hand. To pick a starting point, hold your arm at 90 degrees. Have your training partner watch the range of motion in your arm swing. If you are alone, walk by a storefront and watch your reflection. Otherwise, you will have to estimate your arm swing.

The following figure shows a walker with his arms too far in front and behind his body.

If the angle of your arm swing is too great, your arms will take too long to move forward and back. To improve your arm motion, shorten it. Since your legs and hips can't move faster than your arms, they will be forced to slow down if you do not reduce the angle of your arms.

In contrast, the following figure shows a walker with his arms too close to his body. If the length of your arm swing is too short, your stride length will decrease to compensate. Therefore, you want to increase the angle of your arms.

The following figure depicts the proper range of motion for your arms.

Proper arm swing

The angle at which you are holding your arms should remain constant throughout the arm swing. Opening and closing your arm angle during each stride is a needless waste of energy.

When your arms swing forward, they should follow the same path as when shaking someone's hand. This is shown in the following figure.

Try not to cross your arms too far over your chest as shown in the following diagram. Aside from looking like a chicken, you are directing your effort from side to side, a wasted motion.

If you are bringing your arms too far to the side, an exercise you might try is to brush your arms against the side of your body as you bring them forward and back. Then move your arm out just a hair, so it no longer rubs against your body. Although this is not the perfect location, it is a good starting point.

Another incorrect arm motion is to carry your arms in a straight forward and back motion as shown in the following figure. This will make walking with a smooth style difficult and should be avoided.

Hand position

Relax your hands, but do not allow them to dangle or flop with your arm swing. Your wrist should be straight while your hand should be held in a loose fist with your fingertips facing your hips as the arm swings past. If you are having trouble holding your hand relaxed, make a fist, hold it loosely, then place your thumb between your index finger and your middle finger.

Arm Fatigue

As you work out, your arms or shoulders may get fatigued. If this happens, relax your arms, lower them to your side, and shake them for two or three seconds. Then continue as usual. This will improve circulation, stretch out the muscles and help you to continue walking comfortably. If you want, adding a light upper-body weight program after you walk may help. It's easy to underestimate how much effort it takes to hold your arm in one position for a couple of hours. When one of the authors walks a long distance and he is not in great shape, his biceps will often get sore.

A last check

As a last check of the arms, walk the same way you have been, but lower your elbows as if to drag them on the ground. Did your shoulders lower in the process? If so, use this visualization as a method to help relax your shoulders. Remember, they should be as low as possible.

PROPER POSTURE

Many instructors start their athletic walking lessons with posture, but we usually complete our lessons with it. While good posture is very important, people usually fall into two categories. Either they follow common sense and have reasonably correct posture, or they have walked their whole life with an incorrect posture that takes a long time to correct. To maximize efficiency and reduce potential injuries, we will concentrate on perfecting it.

The principle of good athletic walking posture is simple. Your body should be straight up and down throughout the entire stride. Many people walk with improper posture because they have been coached into bad form. "Get your lean," was a quote often heard from coaches. When their athletes leaned, they naturally leaned forward from the waist. Since this moves the hips backward, the coaches said that you should be leaning forward from the ankles. But this too, is biomechanically incorrect.

Observe the restricted hip position

If you try to lean forward from the ankles throughout your stride, your abdominal and back muscles will have to support your body rather than letting your spine do it. If you try to lean forward from the ankles only on toe-off, but not when your leg passes under your body, then you would have to straighten your torso on each stride. This would cause the body to rock forward and back. This constant swaying would be a waste of energy.

Improper Technique

In contrast, the proper technique can now be seen showing a constant (lack of) lean forward.

Proper Technique

In the 1996 Olympics, Michael Johnson set a world record sprinting 200 meters. Johnson breaks the traditional mold of sprinters. He does not lean forward, rather maintains a straight up and down posture, similar to the technique we teach in athletic walking. He does not lean forward as many advocates of the inefficient form of race walking promote. Many promoters of the forward lean would cite traditional sprinters' form as an example of why we should walk with the same posture. Walking and sprinting are two totally different biomechanical activities and should not be compared in this manner, even when one can make rationalizations (Johnson's case) that we are teaching the right technique.

Sway back

You may still hear a knowledgeable coach tell someone to lean forward, but it is not because the coach is trying to achieve the inefficient style exhibited earlier. On the contrary, the coach is probably trying to correct a backward lean that a walker may be exhibiting. This backward lean causes more of a walker's mass to be behind his hips, as if the walker is carrying a weight. It will slow down his/her forward progress.

Head position

Many novice walkers, instead of looking ahead, look at the ground five feet in front of them. This causes the neck to bend and stresses the neck and shoulders. Eventually this stress may lead to cramps in the neck and shoulders.

A walker should look ahead, not at the ground. Often walkers claim that they are making sure that they don't trip. By looking ahead, you should be able to prevent tripping. Another excuse for improper head position is that the walker is watching his/her form. While it may be necessary to look at your feet some of the time, this should be minimized.

IMPROVING LOWER LEG STYLE

When learning walking techniques, it is best if someone can watch you walk, but often a knowledgeable person or training partner is not available. If you have to, you can use yourself as a coach. Walk in front of glass storefronts and watch your reflection. Make sure you walk far enough away so you can see your whole body. If you walk too close, your reflection will pass by too quickly and you won't be able to see much. Observe how you carry your leg throughout your stride. Look to see if your leg is straightening and how far in front of your body your foot is hitting the ground.

Lower leg carriage

Before we introduce techniques to improve your athletic walking style, here is a quick review of what you have learned so far about how to move your lower legs.

> When walking, place your foot in front of your body, landing on the heel. Your foot should land on either side of an imaginary line, and your toe should be at a 45-degree angle from the ground. Land with your leg straight, and keep it straight until the body has passed over the leg.

Understanding the basic motion of the lower legs gives you a strong foundation to improve upon. The goal is to improve lower leg efficiency, so you want to remove any effort that does not help your body move forward.

First, observe the position and direction of the knee and foot once your rear foot has lifted off the ground. By moving your leg forward, you are helping your body move forward. Up-and-down body motion is required only to help your leg get off and back onto the ground in as straight a line as possible. So avoid any unnecessary upward, downward, or side to side movement. When your rear foot lifts off the ground, it should come forward without rising more than an inch or two off the ground. As your foot swings under your body, it should be almost parallel with the ground. This is shown in the fourth figure in *Proper Lower Leg Style* on the following page. Notice the fourth figure in *Improper Lower Leg Style* on the following page has his foot at an angle with the ground so that his heel is much higher than his toe. Make sure that you are not walking with this improper technique.

In addition, concentrate on keeping the knee as low to the ground as possible. High knee and foot carriage can make you appear to be galloping forward. Aside from being less efficient, this form also will make it appear that you are running.

While one of the definitions of walking is that you must maintain unbroken contact with the ground, there can be a great deal of variance in a walker's style while obeying this rule. The figure below shows the proper knee and foot placement throughout the stride. The knee and foot are not lifted significantly. Notice as the foot swings forward, it is never more than an inch off the ground.

Proper Lower Leg Style

The following picture shows the stride progression of a walker who has high knee drive and high foot carriage. In particular, pay attention to the placement of the knee and foot in the third and fourth positions.

Improper Lower Leg Style

Leaving your foot on the ground

Many walkers lift the rear foot off the ground earlier than is optimum for efficient athletic walking technique, as seen in the following diagrams. Compare the walker who keeps his foot on the ground longer with the one who does not. Note the different distance covered with each stride.

Leaving your rear foot on the ground longer helps because:

1. Your hips are allowed to pivot, which lengthens the stride before your swinging leg touches the ground.
2. The hip muscles that are used to swing the leg forward are stretched, resulting in a reflex that pulls the leg forward faster. The faster-moving swing leg propels your body forward with a greater force, allowing you to pick up speed .
3. Your body exerts a force against the ground due to gravity. When you are standing still, this force is completely vertical. By keeping the foot on the ground longer, the ground reactive force of the body's weight will be more horizontal than vertical, when you lift your heel and move to toe-off. This helps to maintain contact with the ground, while helping to propel the body forward.

Toe off and a final push

You can improve your walking stride if you do not allow your foot to be passively pulled off the ground. By pushing off on your big toe just before it breaks contact with the ground, you add additional effort into your stride. The sensation that you should feel is a flick against the ground. You should feel as if you're floating, a sensation you feel because you are less mechanical and your movements are flowing forward. Pushing too hard results in overstriding and loss of contact with the ground.

Correct Push off

Be sure your push-off results in your body being propelled forward and not upward. If you start to push too soon, your body will be pushed upward as shown in the following figure.

Incorrect Push off

Foot placement

A final consideration in improving your walking style is the action your foot makes when it hits the ground. On heel contact, many novice athletic walkers are not as efficient as they might be. These walkers can be broken into three different groups.

Diggers

The goal of efficient athletic walking technique is to place the foot on the ground with a minimum of force on impact. *Diggers* will strike the ground with excessive force, thus digging their feet into the ground. This has the opposite effect of what you want. By landing hard, you are wasting energy and adding stress to your body that can lead to injuries.

Goose steppers

These walkers take too lofty a stride and let their feet dangle in the air. See the third position in the following diagram. When the foot is dangling, it is neither pushing nor pulling the body forward. This wastes time the body could be using to gain forward momentum. It may also give you the appearance of "lifting," one of the race walking violations. Additionally, once the leg is floating, it must come down. This downward movement adds another unnecessary stress to the stride.

Sliders

Some walkers drag their feet forward as they walk. Aside from wearing your shoes out quickly, the additional contact with the ground will slow your pace. Also, it is easy to trip as your foot slides forward.

Correction for Improper Heel Contact

If you are walking with as efficient technique as possible, each foot contact will be as quiet as possible. To avoid these contact problems the solution is very simple:

1. Listen to your footsteps. If they are noisy, you are wasting energy.
2. Make sure that you are not overstriding.
3. Check for excessive shoe wear.

WALKING THE VARIED ROAD

So far we have explained how to walk athletically, but all of the techniques explained so far assume that you are walking on a flat surface. In the real world, this is not always the case. Although most of the techniques remain the same, some must be modified slightly when traversing uneven surfaces.

Hills

How many times have you walked on a hill that seems to never end? This phenomenon is especially true if you walk on the same hill more than once in a workout or race. While most walkers view a hill as similar to another word that only differs from hill by one vowel, learning to walk properly on a hill minimizes the pain associated with it.

One of the reasons walkers have trouble with hills is that it is much more difficult for athletic walkers to maintain proper form than it is for runners or healthwalkers. For this reason, race walk competitions are seldom held on hilly courses. However, when we work out, we often do not have the luxury of flattening out the neighborhood, so we must learn to cope with it.

Walking athletically uphill requires a slightly different technique than walking on a level surface or downhill. One variation in stride that we have found extremely helpful, especially in competition, is to do the opposite of the obvious. Most people attack up the hill trying to maintain speed, then relax going downhill.

We have found that if you try to maintain effort up and down hill, you will finish the hill much more refreshed. As an added benefit, if you do not *relax* on the downhill, you will come off the hill with more speed. An analogy we like to use is the one of an old car's cruise control. Unlike today's modern cars, which maintain an exact speed as you go over hills, older cars maintained a constant gas level. Therefore, as you traveled up a hill you slowed down, and as you traveled down a hill you accelerated. Like the old car's cruise control, by maintaining effort you are more efficient.

Uphill

To athletically walk uphill, you should imagine yourself a bicycle rider in the lowest gear. Bike riders "spin" their wheels quickly in a gear without a great deal of resistance to move forward efficiently. To get the same effect, shorten your stride. A shorter stride will reduce the effort required per stride. This will help counteract the extra effort needed to climb the hill. Also, don't worry about pushing off with your toe as you would on flat ground. Try to increase the cadence of your legs to compensate for the shorter stride. This will help you maintain a speed closer to your normal stride.

Downhill

Once you hit the crest of the hill and head down, you need to shift gears as a bicycle rider would. Elongate your stride, emphasize the hips, and slow your turnover rate a bit. Do this by exploiting the flexibility in the hips. Let gravity be your friend and allow it to pull you down the hill. For an added surge of speed, allow your swinging leg to attack the ground in front of you. It is true that we mentioned a braking action that slows you down when you overstride. However, the angle caused by walking downhill removes most of it.

A final note of **caution:** If the hill is too steep for you to maintain proper technique comfortably without stress to your knees and body, either jog or slowly healthwalk down the hill. If you are training to race, don't worry about having to train for a hill like that; it won't be in a competitive race walk. If steep hills were placed in races, too many people would be walking illegally down them.

Crowns

While it is obvious to most walkers when they are walking up or down a hill, there is another uneven surface that can cause a walker problems: crowns. Crowns are crests on roads that cause the road to be uneven all the way across. Many roads were intentionally crowned to prevent puddles from forming. While this helps the cars, it can severely hinder an athletic walker. As your foot continually lands on a road with a crown in it, your foot must compensate for the improper footing. Over time, this can lead to an injury.

Choose your roads carefully. Try to walk where there is a sidewalk or no crown in the road. If you must walk on roads that have a crown, try to pick the ones with the least crown. If you have to walk on a crown, walk half your workout with the crown on one side of your body, and then turn around onto the same side of the road for the second half of your workout. This will require that you walk against and with traffic, so be very careful. The author often walks straight down the middle of a road with a crown, but only when the road is lightly traveled and there is good visibility for oncoming cars.

TRAINING

COACHING THE ATHLETIC WALKER

Whether you have a traditional coach or are using this book as your "coach," the first step in training is to make a commitment. Have you decided you want to train as an athlete? Have you decided that you are willing to work at improving your fitness by walking? If so, you will be "on our team." Our team does not require you to be a gifted athlete. Instead, it requires you to have what every gifted athlete has, a commitment to a goal. You must be disciplined and willing to work at being the best you can.

HOW DO YOU TRAIN?

To become an athletic walker, you must understand some basic training principles. First, you have to walk like one, repeating tasks to learn them. Improvement comes when you progress from simple tasks to harder ones. But you cannot progress linearly from one task to another. You will have to adapt to each skill level as you work at it, master it, and then progress to the next level. To accomplish this, you will need to recover between daily bouts of exercise and during the year after long periods of training.

Walk Don't Run!

The more work you do that copies the style of athletic walkers, the more you will be able to walk faster and get into better shape. Running and only occasionally walking like an athlete will make you only an *occasionally trained* athletic walker. Specificity of exercise, the first training principle, requires that **you must walk when you train.** All walking workouts and any drills and exercises that you practice should seek to incorporate the best walking technique your body can manage. Practicing as an athletic walker will make you one. You will develop your own style, utilizing a technique that is very efficient, graceful, and powerful. If you don't practice athletic walking, you won't be an athletic walker.

Practicing biomechanical skills of balance, power, and efficiency, world champion race walkers work on technique drills that perfect the skills that they use when they race. When they drill, they exaggerate and reinforce previously learned skills. When they do so, they walk as efficiently as possible, as if on automatic pilot, as if they have been programmed to walk that way. Good athletes appear to use less effort. They are much more graceful than beginners, and we assume them to be "naturals." Why? Because they have worked at mastering the skills required to perform at their level.

Many champions, in all sports, talk about being in the "zone" when they compete. Many great track and field athletes are not able to remember much about their races when asked about it after they have finished. One of the co-author's athletes was asked immediately after she had finished, in what then would have been an American record, if she could remember the route the athletes took leaving the Rome stadium. She could not. In fact she only remembered one moment, when she was having self-doubts and she had to "trigger" positive thoughts. She was in a trance-like state. She was denied the record because the course could not be verified for the segment leaving the stadium, but the point is, how was she able to walk so well, if not thinking about it? Why do most elite athletes look so graceful? Picture Michael Jordan playing basketball or Michael Johnson running 200 meters at world record pace. Do they remember? They sure look good. They sure do make it look easy. Why? After endless repetition, they do not have to think about their sport. So go out and practice.

Repetition

To get better, simply practice. Over and over. To practice a musical instrument correctly, you have to play scales and then chords. Over and over. To learn how to drive, you had to learn to parallel park. To do so you had to practice. Over and over. The same is true with athletic walking, so go out and practice your sport.

Give Your Body a Chance

To improve strength and endurance, skills must be repeated over and over, but at more difficult work levels. However, since the body will break down under constant increased levels of stress, it must be given opportunities to adapt to the demands that have been placed on it. Unlike a well-oiled machine, that can go on forever, the human body needs to repair itself. It needs to grow anew in order to continue to work. Athletes take breaks to recover from harder work loads. It is during these breaks that the body actually adapts to stress and strengthens itself to be capable of handling more stress in the future. In essence, days off are just as important as days on.

World class and nationally ranked athletes follow the concept of periodization in their yearly training. They include a month-long period of rest once a year. When you begin an athletic walking training program, plan to take one month off during the year. You should stay active, but stay away from walking. Ride a bike, swim, jog (easily if your body can handle it), etc. but stay away from walking hard. It is then, during rest, when the body becomes renewed and refreshed. Research shows that injury and staleness are prevented because of these and other periods of reduced workloads.

Applying the principle of recovery to monthly training cycles, one week per month should be easier than the other three. This will allow you to walk harder, at a higher level, in the next cycle. During your weekly training cycle, it is best to work hard every other day, following a hard/easy approach. That way, your body will adapt to the stress you put on it. If you don't incorporate recovery breaks, you will break down! Overtraining results in staleness, a feeling of "blah!" leading you to feel like, "I don't want to train today." Often times, overtrained athletes get injured or they become ill. Being overtrained will take more time to overcome than the amount of time "lost" if you had rested. If you do not heed this simple advice, watch out for it. Take time off, and it wouldn't hurt to take a vacation as well.

SETTING UP A TRAINING PROGRAM

When you start doing conditioning work, you must train the various systems that you will use when you seek to walk faster or farther. You need to train specifically to achieve your goals. It will not pay to do lots of short sprints, if you want to prepare for a long endurance walk. Conversely, walking slowly all the time will not help you get faster.

So the first step is to decide what your goal is as an athletic walker. Do you merely want to learn the technique? Do you want to see how fast you can walk in a race? Do you want to walk a marathon? There are plenty of running races that you walk, particularly if you walk fast (which you will do walking like an athlete). You might even want to try your skill and style in a judged race walk. What your goal is matters.

The Conversation Test.

If you want to simply learn the athletic walking technique, or if you are just beginning a training program, you need to walk for periods of time that exceed 20 to 30 minutes. You should walk in a relaxed, easy fashion, but what does it mean to walk easy? If you can carry on a conversation, and you do not seem bothered by talking to the people you are training with, you are probably training at a easy level. Sometimes walks go on for hours with no effort. Conversation is pleasant.

Aerobic vs. Anaerobic Exercise

When you are walking at an easy level, you are walking aerobically. Aerobic means to train in the presence of oxygen. The blood stream gets sufficient oxygen to process blood sugars into energy, and your body removes waste products from this process without creating lactic acid (a byproduct of working without enough oxygen).

When you are walking harder, you feel tired, but can still gab up a storm. You still are walking aerobically, but at a harder level. On the other hand, if you are breathing harder and feel somewhat annoyed by conversation, as in, "I'll talk to you later," you have crossed over to anaerobic exercise and your body is producing lactic acid in the process. Lactic acid causes muscles to fatigue. If you can't talk at all because you are panting so hard and you want to bend over to catch your breath, you have worked at a high anaerobic level.

Beginning and intermediate walkers train aerobically. Training aerobically can be easy or be moderately hard. When training harder aerobically, you work harder, but you do not cross over to anaerobic training.

Monitoring Your Pulse

A simple way to be a little more precise is to stop and take your pulse (Some athletes use a heart rate monitor while they exercise, avoiding having to stop and stand still). You can easily find the pulse at your wrist or your neck if you have been exercising for a few moments. Use your index and middle finger to count the number of heartbeats per minute. Do not use your thumb or you will get an inaccurate reading. Counting for 10 seconds will give you a good idea. You have to multiply by 6 to get 60 seconds worth of heartbeats. (Some athletes count for 6 seconds and then add a 0 to the count, but this is slightly less accurate.) The higher your pulse, the harder you are working.

What Should Your Pulse Be?

To calculate the desired range of your heart rate during easy to moderate aerobic exercise, you need to calculate an expected "maximum" pulse rate for your age. A standard formula is to subtract your age from the number 220. That, in the absence of more sophisticated testing in a lab, is your maximum. While this method is not effective for trained athletes, it is a good starting place for beginners. Normally, we would calculate your heart range for easy to moderate aerobic exercise as 65% to 80% of your maximum. Since we are using an estimated maximum, we are going to modify this calculation using the Karvonen method. To get a more accurate estimate of the range, we must calculate your resting heart rate. Your resting heart rate is your pulse when you first awaken in the morning.

Now you have all the information you need to calculate your estimated range:

(220 - age - resting heart rate) X .65 + resting heart rate
to
(220 - age - resting heart rate) X .8 + resting heart rate

Here is an example for a 50 year-old whose resting heart rate is 66.
(220 - 50 - 66) X .65 + 66 = 134 beats/minute (lower target range)
(220 - 50 - 66) X .8 + 66 = 149 beats/minute (higher target range)

When you first start to walk like an athlete, no doubt, your pulse will go up quickly. That is normal. Pay attention to your pulse. As you learn the skill, and as you get in better shape, your pulse will not rise as quickly. You will be able to achieve your goal of staying in your target zone longer. That is an indication that you are in better shape.

Getting Started - Basic Aerobic Conditioning

To start athletic walking (after you have received your doctor's permission, if you have been relatively sedentary), work out every other day, with a goal of walking 20 to 30 minutes each session. If you find the technique very taxing or your pulse gets out of your target range, start off walking normally, athletic walking for only short periods of time. The goal is to exercise for at least 30 minutes. Stay at this level for four weeks. This way, you will adapt to the technique and conditioning effort. Every other week will only have three training sessions, which will allow you to recover from the week with four workouts.

Week	Sunday	Monday	Tuesday	Wednesday	Thursday	Friday	Saturday
First	30 min.	off	30 min.	off	30 min.	off	30 min.
Second	off	30 min.	off	30 min.	off	30 min.	off
Third	30 min.	off	30 min.	off	30 min.	off	30 min.
Fourth	off	30 min.	off	30 min.	off	30 min.	off

After this first period, you will be ready to increase the level of your training schedule. Walk two days in a row, and then take a day off. This way, in the first week, you will train five days, and rest two days. On the second, you will train four and rest three. Stay at this level for three weeks. Resist the temptation to do more unless you have already been walking for fitness, because your body must adapt to this work.

Week	Sunday	Monday	Tuesday	Wednesday	Thursday	Friday	Saturday
Fifth	30 min.	30 min.	off	30 min.	30 min.	off	30 min.
Sixth	30 min.	off	30 min.	30 min.	off	30 min.	30 min.
Seventh	off	30 min.	30 min.	off	30 min.	30 min.	off

The seventh week has three resting days, so it is a relatively easy week

Aerobic Endurance

The more aerobic work you do as an athletic walker, the better prepared you will be for further improvement. Even if your goal is to give yourself a time trial (athletes like to see how they are doing against the clock), or if you enter a race (to see how you do against others), most of the effort while testing yourself in this "racing" situation will be done aerobically. To build aerobic endurance, longer walks must be added.

After walking at the introductory amount of 20 to 30 minutes per workout session, increase your distance slightly, adding 15 minutes to every other workout. Eventually, you will want to set a goal of doing one hour as your basic long walk. To get to that level, you must adapt to harder work. (Harder is equated with time on your feet walking aerobically.)

For weeks 8 through 10, add 15 minutes to every other workout, making alternate workouts 45 minutes long. Still take a day off every third day. The 10th week will again be an easy week, because you will have three days off. On the 11th week, work out three days in a row twice. Sandwich two 30-minute walks around a 45-minute session. During the 12th week, a 30-minute walk could be sandwiched between two 45-minute walks during one of the three days of training. On the 13th week, a 60-minute walk could be added at the end of the week.

Week	Sunday	Monday	Tuesday	Wednesday	Thursday	Friday	Saturday
Eighth	45 min.	30 min.	off	45 min.	30 min.	off	45 min.
Ninth	30 min.	off	45 min.	30 min.	off	45 min.	30 min.
Tenth	off	45 min.	30 min.	off	45 min.	30 min.	off
Eleventh	30 min.	45 min.	30 min.	off	30 min.	45 min.	off
Twelfth	45 min.	30 min.	45 min.	off	30 min.	45 min.	30 min.
Thirteenth	off	45 min.	30 min.	45 min.	off	30 min.	60 min.

The variety of workouts can get pretty complicated. Gradually progress to harder workouts, maintaining recovery workouts and days off each week. You may want to add longer walks to your program. When depends on which days you train and the goals you have set for yourself. Try following a long walk with an easy day to start. Eventually, you may not think much of your 30-minute walks. But keep in mind they are better than doing nothing.

Latter Weeks	Sunday	Monday	Tuesday	Wednesday	Thursday	Friday	Saturday
First	45 min.	30 min.	45 min.	off	45 min.	30 min.	45 min.
Second	30 min.	60 min.	30 min.	45 min.	off	30 min.	60 min.
Third	off	45 min.	30 min.	45 min.	30 min.	30 min.	60 min.

Days Off.

When you start to walk, you should walk every other day, resting on the other day. By the time you improve your aerobic endurance so that you can walk beyond one hour, we recommend that you still take a minimum of one day off a week.

Don't feel so compelled to follow a rigid schedule. If the weather is bad and you are not adjusted to it, or if you are feeling worn out, listen to the world around you and adjust accordingly.

Training to Get Fitter, Faster, and For Competition

After you have worked on your aerobic conditioning, and you can train for one hour or more, two or three times a week, and are walking for 20 or 30 minutes the other days, you are ready to add speed training to your program. After all, walking like an athlete will make you faster, capable of turning in vastly improved performances. To do so, you need to get a feel for quickness, the feel for speed associated with racing.

If you want to walk faster, throw in some repeat sprints one day a week. How many depends upon how well you are mastering the athletic walking technique. Some walkers can only hold form for 100 meters, or ¼ of the way around a standard running track. Others may be able to do it halfway, or for a complete lap. Once you start doing this over and over, you are doing what is called doing repeats.

Repeats and Recovery Time.

When you walk repetitions at a moderately easy aerobic level, you do not need to take much rest between each repeat. One to two minutes is plenty. As you walk faster, and breathe harder, see how long it takes to get your breathing back to a comfortable level. Walk the next repeat when your breathing has returned to normal. Your heart will be beating faster, but you will be ready to go. If you use the "conversation" test, you'll say "let's go!" and not want to argue. For longer, harder efforts, recover for ½ the amount of time you took walking the repeat.

Sets.

As you get the feel for the speed, you might want to break your repetitions into sets. Let's say you want to do 12 x 200 meters (halfway around a track), or if you are advancing rapidly, you want to do 12x400 meters (once around a track). Break the repeats into groups such as 3x200 meters, followed by a longer rest period, and then 3x200 meters again until you have completed the number of repetitions you had planned to do. (Make sure you take your planned repeat recovery break in between each 200 meters.)

As you advance, or as you start to incorporate more anaerobic work in your training (say there's a race coming up and you want to be able to tolerate the early pace or you want to prepare for a hard, sustained finish), you might decide to walk the later sets faster, to add more harder-level work. As a rule of thumb, earlier sets should be slower than faster sets. Fatigued muscles have a hard time getting rid of waste products and will not operate aerobically with lactic acid in them, so do the easier aerobic repetitions first, and then move on to harder anaerobic work if you want.

Longer Repetitions.

When you get in shape, you may think about doing longer repetitions, such as one mile, or something similar. Doing these will bring you to the anaerobic threshold during your walk. Remember the conversation test when you do these. It is important to try to maintain a constant speed throughout the repetition. Many beginners will walk very quickly for the 1st ¼ mile, only to slow down significantly for the remainder of the mile.

Three or more long repeats are tough to do. You may not want to talk during later laps around a track or over your training course, but while recovering, you'll be saying to yourself and others, "That was great. Let's do another!" Long repeats sure do make you mentally tough. They give you power. What you will be doing is making yourself able to work aerobically without going anaerobic. What used to put you near exhaustion will be now be efficient.

You're First Race

If you wish to compete, once you've incorporated longer repetitions into your workout, you are ready to enter a 5K or 10K race. Read over the *Mental Preparation* section to help alleviate any pre-race jitters. Don't worry about finishing last, by using the techniques in this book you won't be. Just make sure that you get to the race early enough to warm up and stretch properly.

Advanced Training for Racing

Once you've mastered the techniques of athletic walking, you may want to train for competition, but where do you begin? You must decide on a realistic goal, plan a training program for racing, and follow it. This training program is designed for people who have already mastered the techniques in this book and are able to walk for at least 1½ hours at a time at least twice a week.

When training for competition, you set up a periodization plan similar to the one that follows. It is divided into four periods of training. Each is designed to train a different energy system. The schedule is set up for an entire year, but you may not have that much time to prepare. If this is true, pick your training up at an appropriate time, or shorten the periods somewhat. This way you will cover all of the training phases. Notice that the schedule, as a whole, does not contain a lot of races early. Do not be tempted to race too often. Racing every weekend can lead to poor performances and injury.

Picking a Goal

Before you design a training program you must first pick a realistic goal. If you are currently walking at 15-minute mile pace, setting your goal pace (GP) at 10 minutes/mile is unrealistic.

To calculate goal pace, select the distance you want to train for, such as 5 kilometers (3.1 miles) or 10 kilometers (6.2 miles). This plan is based on a goal of 10 kilometers for an intermediate walker. Estimate a realistic completion time, and then divide that time by the distance called for in the training schedule.

First Period - Base Period - Longer Aerobic Endurance

The first period is often referred to as the base period. This is the time of year that you should be working on easy (aerobic) walking. Your walking should be done while being able to maintain a comfortable conversation. The only workout during the week that is at a quicker pace is Wednesdays. However, you should still be able to maintain a comfortable conversation while walking it as well.

Week	Sunday	Monday	Tuesday	Wednesday	Thursday	Friday	Saturday
1	9 miles	5 miles	5 miles	2x2mi @ GP+ 120sec.	8 miles	off	5 miles
2	10 miles	"	"	"	"	"	"
3	11 miles	"	"	"	"	"	"
4	12 miles	"	"	5 miles	"	"	"
5	10 miles	"	"	2x2mi @ GP+100sec.	"	"	"
6	11 miles	"	6 miles	"	"	"	6 miles
7	12 miles	"	"	"	"	"	"
8	13 miles	"	"	5 miles	"	"	"
9	11 miles	"	"	3x 2mi @ GP + 100 sec	"	"	"
10	12 miles	"	"	"	"	"	"
11	13 miles	"	"	"	"	"	"
12	14 miles	"	"	"	"	"	"

Base Period Training Schedule

Wednesday's workout may need further explanation. 2x2mi @ GP + 120 seconds means that you should do the following:

> First, warm up by walking one to two miles at an easy pace. Make sure that you have stretched well. Then walk two miles at your goal pace + 120 seconds. If your goal pace for a 10K is 10-minute miles, then you should walk the two miles in 22 minutes.

> Then take three to four minutes rest, long enough that you are breathing comfortably. Then do another 22 minute - two mile walk.

> Finally warm down for a mile or so and stretch, stretch, stretch.

Notice that Sunday's workout cycles. Over a series of weeks, for the first three weeks the mileage walked increases by one, then you drop back a few miles and start the cycle again. Each time you drop down the distance, you do not drop all the way back. This is a sensible approach to increasing your mileage. If you do not cycle back, you will not give your body a chance to adapt to the increased workload. Usually, each time you cycle back, you will be able to increase your pace a little bit without increasing your exertion level. Do not increase the speed so much that you are no longer able to carry on a comfortable conversation.

Building Power and Economy - Anaerobic Threshold Training

We stated earlier that you will walk the majority of your race aerobically. One of the goals in training is to condition the body so that it can work harder and remain in an aerobic mode. To accomplish this, you must walk at levels that approach your anaerobic threshold, where you no longer find it pleasant to talk, even a little. We accomplish this by increasing the pace of our repetition workout and changing our Thursday workout from easy distance, to working just below the anaerobic threshold. You can pick up the pace of your easy distance walks a little bit, but do not allow them to approach the level that you are walking on Tuesdays or Thursdays.

Week	Sunday	Monday	Tuesday	Wednesday	Thursday	Friday	Sat.
1	9 miles	6 miles	4 x 1 mile @ GP + 20 sec.	8 miles	4 miles just below AT	Off	6 miles
2	10 miles	"	"	"	"	"	"
3	11 miles	"	"	"	"	"	"
4	12 miles	"	5 miles easy	"	"	"	"
5	9 miles	"	5 x 1 mile @ GP + 20 sec.	"	5 miles just below AT	"	"
6	10 miles	"	"	"	"	"	"
7	11 miles	"	"	"	"	"	"
8	12 miles	"	5 miles easy	"	"	"	"
9	9 miles	"	6 x 1 mile @ GP + 20 sec	"	"	"	"
10	10 miles	"	"	"	"	"	"
11	11 miles	"	"	"	6 miles just below AT	"	"
12	12 miles	"	5 miles easy	"	"	"	"
13	9 miles	"	6 x1 mile 2 @GP+20sec 2 @GP+10sec 2 @ GP	"	"	"	"
14	10 miles	"	"	"	"	"	"
15	11 miles	"	"	"	"	"	"
16	12 miles	"	"	"	"	"	"

Power and Economy Training Schedule

Tuesday's workout may need further explanation. 4x1mi @ GP + 20 seconds means that you should do the following:

> First, warm up by walking one to two miles at an easy pace. Make sure that you have stretched well. Then walk one mile at your goal pace + 20 seconds. If your goal pace for a 10K is 10-minute miles, then you should walk the one mile in 10 minutes and 20 seconds.

> Then take three to four minutes rest, long enough that you are breathing comfortably. Then do the remainder of the miles in the same

fashion. As the number of repeats increases, you will be getting in better and better shape. Toward the end of the cycle you will also increase the pace to be at your goal pace.

Finally warm down for a mile or so and stretch, stretch, stretch.

Notice every few weeks you will take a break from repetitions. This will give your body a chance to recover and rebuild itself. Thursday's workouts are simple. Warm up for a mile and then walk the prescribed distance at a level (just below your anaerobic threshold) where it is uncomfortable to talk, but not impossible. Then warm down.

Early Season Competition

As you get closer to your goal race, you will reduce your overall weekly mileage walked, increase the pace of your repetition workouts, and begin to race. You will be walking the majority of your anaerobic workouts in this period.

Week	Sunday	Monday	Tuesday	Wednesday	Thursday	Friday	Saturday
1	Time Trial	6 miles	2x1mi @	5 miles	10x400m	6 miles	8 miles
2	9 miles	"	10km GP	"	at @GP	6 miles	8 miles
3	10 miles	"	4x 800m @	"	5 miles	3 miles	off
4	Minor Race	"	5km GP	"	12x400m	6 miles	8 miles
5	9 miles	"	4x 400m	"	@ GP	6 miles	8 miles
6	10 miles	"	@ 5k GP	"	5 miles	3 miles	off
7	Race	"	- 5 seconds	"	12x 400m	6 miles	8 miles
8	9 miles	"		"	@ GP - 5 sec	6 miles	8 miles
9	10 miles	"	12x 400 m	"	5 miles	3 miles	off
10	Race	"	1-4@GP	"	12x 400m @ GP - 5 sec	6 miles	8 miles
11	9 miles	"	5-8@GP-5sec	"		6 miles	8 miles
12	10 miles	"	9-12@ all out	"	5 miles	3 miles	off

Early Season Competition Training Schedule

Tuesday's workout will be a series of repetitions that are much quicker than previous repetitions. The first eight weeks, you will do a combination of repetitions that are longer, while the last four weeks, you will do only ¼ mile repetitions, but done at a much faster pace.

Thursday's workouts will cycle every three weeks. Two weeks you will walk ¼ mile repetitions, and the third week you will walk an easy 5-mile workout. Each time we start the cycle over you will either increase the number of repetitions or the speed at that you are walking them.

CHAMPIONSHIP SEASON

The culmination of the year's hard work is the championship season. Over a few weeks, you fine-tune your body to reach a peak performance. During this time you can race a couple of times, but it is impossible to maintain a peak for a long period of time. So, plan your important races together. Notice that your weekly mileage total is much lower than the previous cycles. Your work is done-you can't get in shape in the last weeks if you haven't already done the right workouts.

Week	Sunday	Monday	Tuesday	Wednesday	Thursday	Friday	Saturday
1	Race	5 miles	8 x 400m @ GP	off	5 miles	off	5 miles
2	6 miles	5 miles	8 x 400m @ GP	off	6 straights	off	2 miles
3	Race	5 miles	8 x 400m @ GP	off	6 straights	off	2 miles
4	Race						

Championship Season Training Schedule

All distance other than your races and repetitions should be at a easy, comfortable pace. When doing your repetitions at your goal pace, you will be getting used to your race pace. This way, when you start to walk your race, your pace will be familiar. These repetition workouts should feel fairly easy and walked aerobically, after all, you have trained to make your race pace an aerobic activity. Thursday's workout is designed to loosen you up before your race. Warm up for a mile or so. Then walk the straight section of the track at your race pace. Walk the curved section of the track slowly. Then repeat this six times. Then warm down about a mile.

Active Rest

After your championship season is over, it is important to incorporate a period of active rest. For the next month, you should not do any athletic walking. Don't worry about getting out of shape, your body needs this time to rebuild itself. When you start the training cycle again, you will be well rested and ready to improve to your next goal.

Rest Period	1-2 weeks	No training. Complete Rest
Active Rest	2-3 weeks	Cross Training. Hiking, Biking, Swimming, Jogging

STRETCHING

One of the most neglected components of exercise, stretching, prevents injuries and feels good. Due to time constraints, we often neglect stretching and concern ourselves only with getting our scheduled mileage completed. If you are tempted to make this compromise, don't. Sacrifice one mile of your workout and make sure you stretch properly.

Stretching can prevent injuries. Don't learn this the hard way. If you do not stretch properly, you will lose more mileage because of injuries than the few miles you will miss taking the time to stretch. Some of the stretches detailed are common to many forms of exercise, while others are unique to walking.

While we list many possible stretches, it is not necessary for you to do every one every day. Some are for beginners, while others are only for more advanced walkers. We recommend that you select at least one stretch for each group of muscles. Also, it is a good idea to stretch on your days off from walking. This will allow your body to be more fully recovered for your next workout.

Take your time while stretching. Make sure that you are using good technique. Improper form will lead to stretching the wrong group of muscles. Generally, unless otherwise noted, all stretches should be held for 20-30 seconds. When stretching, do not bounce in an attempt to stretch a little more. You need stretch only far enough to feel your muscles elongating. After all, the goal is not to stretch until it hurts, but to warm up the muscles and prepare them for exercise.

Contrary to popular belief, stretching before you walk is not recommended. If you stretch without exercising at all, you are stretching cold muscles, which is less effective. Instead, begin your exercise routine by walking a little bit at a very leisurely pace to warm up and get the blood flowing through your muscles, then follow with your stretches. After walking, you should stretch again to help minimize any chance of injury.

Often when starting an exercise program, it is difficult to remember everything that you need to do. That is why we recommend stretching from the bottom of your body and up. This helps you from forgetting what stretches you have already done.

The first stretches we will discuss are for the major muscle groups in the legs. It is especially important in athletic walking to stretch every muscle group, because you are going to use each of these muscle groups to walk faster and get a better overall workout. For those who are not familiar with the names of the different muscle groups, we have included the following diagram.

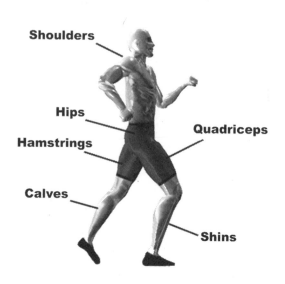

CALF STRETCHES

In walking, especially when using the techniques we will explain, your calf muscles are used considerably more than in other sports. Therefore, we have included four different calf stretches. Each works a slightly different area of the calf. Therefore, if you have the time, do them all; it will not be overkill.

Traditional Calf Stretch

The first stretch is probably the most common of the calf stretches.

Place both hands, at shoulder height, on a wall in front of your body. Keep your arms fairly straight and one leg a little bent under your body. Now, with your toe pointed to the ground, place the other leg about 1 1/2 to 2 feet behind your body.

While keeping your rear leg fairly straight and without moving its position, place the heel of your rear foot on the ground. You should feel a stretch down the outer part of your calf muscle. If you don't, try to move your rear leg back a little farther. Throughout the stretch, keep your upper body vertical; make sure you do not bend forward.

Advanced Calf Stretch

If your calves are extremely flexible, the *Traditional Calf Stretch* may not be very helpful because it stretches the calves only a little bit. Therefore, you may want to try this more advanced calf stretch and the others that follow, which we personally find more effective.

The *Advanced Calf Stretch* is actually the simplest calf stretch, but because it stretches much more aggressively than the *Traditional Calf Stretch*, it should be done only by more advanced walkers.

You will need to find a step or a curb with a tree or pole nearby. Use the pole to maintain your balance throughout the stretch. If something to lean against is not readily available, you might try using another walker to help maintain your balance. Place your toes as close to the edge of the step as you can while maintaining your balance.

While keeping your legs straight, lower your heels as much as possible. You should feel the stretch in your calves. To stretch your calves more, try moving your feet farther off the edge of the curb. You can also stretch your calf further by lowering only one leg at a time. You can place the leg you are not stretching wherever you want, but be careful to maintain your balance.

Most Aggressive Calf Stretch

The third calf stretch is the most aggressive of the calf stretches discussed. Because it will stretch areas of the calf that are not reached by the less aggressive stretches, it should be done only by more advanced walkers.

The *Most Aggressive Calf Stretch* requires a wall, sign or lamp post to lean against. Walk up to a wall and stand one arm's length away. Place the toes of one foot on the wall itself, as if you stepped onto it. Now place one of your heels as close to the base of the wall as possible. Your foot should have space under it as shown in the figure to the right.

Keep your leg and back straight and lean into the wall slowly. The closer to the wall you are, the more you will stretch your calf. Lean only to the point that you feel a good stretch in your upper calf. Do not stretch until you feel pain. Please note that you will usually feel this stretch higher in the calf than the other calf stretches described so far. This stretch is demonstrated using one leg at a time. It can also be done stretching both legs at a time, but this is a little more difficult.

Bent Leg Calf Stretch

The fourth calf stretch may feel like less of a stretch than the others, but it is still very important. Many of us do not realize that the calf is not a single muscle, but two. All the stretches so far are used to stretch the outer calf muscle. To completely stretch the calf muscles, we need to stretch the inner calf as well. This can be accomplished with the *Bent Leg Calf Stretch.*

The *Bent Leg Calf Stretch* starts in the position in which you ended the *Traditional Calf Stretch.* Place both hands, at shoulder height, on a wall in front of your body. Keep your arms fairly straight and one leg a little bent under your body. Now, with your toe pointed to the ground, place the other leg about 1 1/2 to 2 feet behind your body. While keeping your rear leg fairly straight and without moving its position, place the heel of your rear foot on the ground.

Bend your rear leg while keeping your foot on the ground. Make sure you keep your entire foot, especially the heel, on the ground. You will feel this stretch deeper in your calf muscle. It will not feel as pronounced as the other stretches, but it works.

SHIN STRETCH

Most people stretch their calves but completely neglect the opposite muscles in the shin. You use your shins much more in walking than in other activities. When you walk, you land on your heel and point your toe. This requires the use of your shin muscles in a way in which your body is not normally accustomed. Therefore, it is very important to stretch your shins. This will help prevent shin splints.

To stretch your shins, balance yourself near a wall or post. Put your weight on one leg and straighten it. Now, point your other foot to the ground, toe first. With your toe touching the ground, roll this foot forward, so that your toenail is almost touching the ground. Move your leg forward from the ankle.

You should feel a stretch in your shin. If you don't, try again after you finish walking. After walking you will have worked your shin muscles and they will be tighter than before the walk. If you don't feel the stretch even after walking, read this section over again, because you may be performing the stretch improperly. Some people feel this stretch more when doing it without shoes.

HAMSTRING STRETCHES

There are endless ways to stretch the hamstring. We will present a few. If you have one that you are comfortable with, you may choose to continue to use it.

Traditional Hamstring Stretch

This stretch is the most traditional of the stretches we will explain. In a seated position, place the leg you want to stretch straight in front of you. Then place the other leg alongside to make a triangle with your legs. This can be seen in the top view shown below.

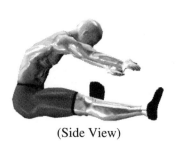

(Side View)

(Top View)

With a straight back, bend from your hips, and lean toward your toes. Reach for your toes with both hands and hold for 20 to 30 seconds. Do not bounce in an attempt to reach your toes. It is OK to not reach them.

Easy on the Back Hamstring Stretch

This stretch is perfect if you have back problems. By lying on your back, you will reduce the stress to your lower back while still adequately stretching the hamstring muscle.

Start by lying on the ground and positioning the leg you are not stretching so that it makes a triangle with the ground. Try to lift the other leg, holding it straight, up to about 90 degrees. Hold this position for 20-30 seconds. If you are very flexible, try to bring your leg even closer to your body.

Repeat this stretch with the other leg.

Dynamic Toe Touching Hamstring Stretch

The first stretch is called a dynamic stretch, because it is done while walking. In the cold winter days, this is often the preferred stretch, because it has the added benefit of allowing your body to warm up while it stretches. However, this stretch should only be done if you don't have back problems. If you have a bad back, stick with some of the other stretches.

Start with one leg straight supporting your weight. Now place the other leg straight in front of you about six inches.

Point the toes of your forward foot, and with your opposite hand, touch your pointed toes. Lower your toes and step with your supporting leg, placing it six inches ahead of the other. Point your toes as before, and touch it with the opposite hand.

Continue to do this and walk about 25 yards. Remember, it is not a race. Speed does not improve stretching. You may reach with either one or two hands, whichever is more comfortable for you.

Dynamic Leg Lifting Hamstring Stretch

A variation of the *Dynamic Toe Touching Hamstring Stretch* is to hold your hand directly in front of your torso at chest height as depicted in the figure to the left.

Walk forward and as you step, lifting each leg up to your corresponding hand. Each step should be as before, only about six inches.

Continue to do this for about 25 yards.

Improved Toe Touching Hamstring Stretch

We all remember being asked to touch our toes in gym class, but what we didn't know is that bending over and touching our toes can cause stress to the lower back. We want to avoid bending over and coming straight down. To avoid the stress, try the *Improved Toe Touching Hamstring Stretch*.

Instead of standing straight up, lean against a wall, pole, or tree. While keeping your buttocks against the wall, place your feet about ½ to 1 foot from the wall.

While keeping contact with the wall, bend down and try to touch your toes. By moving your feet away from the wall, you reduce the lower back strain and help prevent the chance of pulling your sciatic nerve (One of the largest nerves in your body, located in the pelvic region).

Slow Yoga Style Hamstring Stretch

This stretch loosens your hamstrings as well as your back. It is important to do this stretch very slowly. By proceeding slowly through each step of the stretch, you will stretch and relax different areas of the body.

 This stretch starts in the same position as the last hamstring stretch

 Lower just your head so that your chin is tucked toward your chest.

 Now slowly lower your arms and back.

 Now, completely lower your arms and back. Hang as low as you can for 10-20 seconds and then reverse the process.

You should go up as slowly as you came down, with your head being the very last part to come up.

Back-of-the-knee Stretch

Sometimes the back of the knee will get a little sore from walking. In a seated position, place the leg of the knee you want to stretch straight in front of you. Then place the other leg alongside to make a triangle with your legs. (see the figure below from the top view) With a straight back, bend from your hips, and lean toward your toe. Reach for your toe with both hands and hold for 20 to 30 seconds. Now pull your toes toward your body. If you can't reach your toes, use a towel to extend your grasp.

Top View

Side View

Dancer's Stretch

The final hamstring stretch can be done without using a wall or getting on the floor. It is traditionally used by dancers, but it can be very effective for walkers as well.

Stand with both feet together, both legs straight, and your hands at your sides.

Stand, putting your weight on your straightened right leg. Bend your left knee. Keeping your shoulders square, bend down and forward. You should feel the stretch in your hamstring.

(Side View)

For more support, you may place your left hand on your left leg. This will help you prevent yourself from bending your back. As an additional stretch, lift your right toe upward. Repeat this exercise switching legs.

QUADRICEPS STRETCH

The only simple and effective stretch we know of is one that most of you are familiar with.

Standing next to something for balance, raise the leg you want to stretch behind you and grab your foot. The upper part of the leg should remain in a vertical position as you pull your foot upward.

A slight variation in this stretch is to pull your foot back slightly; this will help stretch other areas of the quadriceps.

Be careful not to pull your leg to the side. It may put unneeded stress on your knee. Repeat this stretch for the opposite leg.

HIP STRETCHES

When athletically walking, the hips are used extensively. Stretching them properly will allow a greater range of motion, thereby increasing the effectiveness of the hip motion. Also, stretching the hips will reduce risk of injury.

Curb Hip Stretch

The first stretch is quite simple, but it requires a step or a reasonably high curb and something to balance against.

Stand with one leg on the curb while letting the other leg hang off of it. Now, lower the hanging leg and keep both legs straight. You will feel the stretch on the hip opposite the curb. Repeat the stretch for the other hip.

Seated Hip Stretch

The second hip stretch can be done sitting down on the ground with both legs in front of your body. Cross your right leg over the left leg. Now, take your left hand and pull the right leg to the left and toward the body. You should feel a stretch in your hip. Reverse your legs to stretch your left hip.

GROIN STRETCH

Seated Groin Stretch

When you walk athletically, you may experience tightness in the muscles in the groin area. By regularly practicing the *Seated Groin Stretch*, you can reduce any discomfort you might experience.

Start by sitting down and placing your legs in a diamond shape as depicted in the top view below. Notice in the side view that your legs should be flush against the ground. It is important to keep your legs as low to the ground as possible while doing this stretch.

Front View   Top View   Side View

Now lean forward, keeping your back as straight as possible, and reach for your toes. Hold the position shown in the following figure for 20-30 seconds.

SHOULDER STRETCHES

In athletic walking, you use your arms to move through a larger range of motion than in traditional walking or running. By keeping the shoulders stretched and relaxed, you are much more comfortable and efficient.

Windmill Stretch

The first shoulder stretch, the *Windmill Stretch*, is referenced in many sources. However, many do not show the proper range of motion for the stretch. To maximize its effectiveness, be sure to follow the diagrams carefully.

This stretch should be done slowly. Stand straight up, with your hands at your sides.

Raise your left arm to about 90 degrees from your body.

Continue to raise the arm, but angle it toward your head. As you bring the arm back, try to brush your biceps against your face.

Continue to bring the arm back, rotating it slightly away from the body.

83

Continuation of the Windmill Stretch

 Continue to bring the arm back, and continue rotating it slightly away from the body.

 Bring the arm back to its original position.

Repeat this rotational stretch about ten times with your left arm. Now do the same rotations with your right arm. After you are comfortable with this stretch, try doing both arms at the same time. The arms should be 180 degrees apart: When one arm is above the head, the other arm will be below the waist.

The final evolution of this stretch is to practice it while walking instead of standing still.

Shoulder Stretch 2

This shoulder stretch is similar to the *Windmill Shoulder Stretch* and should be done extremely slowly.

 Start by placing your left arm in the saluting position.

 Lower your left hand so that it touches your shoulder.

 Rotate your left elbow forward, so that your arm is perpendicular with your body.

 Rotate your arm straight up, bringing your arm as close to your face as possible.

Now rotate your arm back and to the side until it is perpendicular to the side of your body.

Continue to rotate your arm back and bring it in closer to your side. Bring the arm up. Now you can bring it back to the position shown to the left.

Most people rush this part of the stretch and do not attain the proper range of motion. You should not simply make circles with your arm. Repeat this exercise for the right arm. Like the *Windmill Shoulder Stretch*, you can do this exercise with both arms simultaneously.

Static Shoulder Stretch

This shoulder stretch should be done while standing. Your goal is to try to clasp your hands behind your head as shown in the following figure.

Hold the stretch for 20-30 seconds, then repeat the stretch switching your arms. Be aware that it is common for you to be more flexible with one arm than the other.

Depending upon your flexibility, you may not be able to clasp your hands. If not, then reach as far as you can, as shown in the figure to the left, or hold a small face towel with each hand. Hold your hands as close together on the towel as you can.

In either case, after holding the stretch for 20-30 seconds, switch arms and repeat.

ADDITIONAL EXERCISES TO HELP YOU WALK

While walking the way we prescribe utilizes 95% of the muscles, you can add a few simple exercises to help prevent injuries and improve walking style. Most can be done at home with little or no weights involved. Done properly, they enhance a walking program.

WRITE THE ALPHABET

One of the simplest, most effective exercises can be done at work. Sit in a chair and try to write each letter of the alphabet with your foot. Keep your toes on the ground and minimize your leg movement. Do this exercise with both feet and you will stretch and strengthen the ankle and shins. If you are bored, you can try spelling out words and phrases. Just do not let your boss catch you making derogatory remarks about him or her.

WALKING ON YOUR TOES

This exercise is done by walking on your toes, taking short strides, keeping your heels as high off the ground as possible. Each stride should be no more than six inches. Walk this way for about 25 yards. If your calves tire quickly, stop walking on your toes briefly and stretch your calves a little. Then complete the rest of the exercise. If 25 yards is really easy, go a little farther.

Remember, it is not a race. You will gain more from doing this exercise slowly than quickly. It is a good idea to do the calf stretching exercises explained earlier after this exercise.

SIMPLE CALF RAISE

This exercise is best done with something to help keep your balance.

This calf exercise is similar to the second calf stretch on page 68. Find a step and position your toes as close to the edge while you can maintain your balance.

Then hang your heels off of the edge and raise them as much as you can. Now lower your heels as low as you can without losing your balance.

Repeat this 10 to 15 times, but be careful not to cheat by leaning your body against whatever you are using for balance.

If you are comfortable, try to do this modification of the simple calf exercise by balancing on one leg at a time.

WALKING ON YOUR HEELS

Your shins and calves are used much more in walking than in other sports, with the possible exception of horseback riding, where the feet are in stirrups. Most people need to strengthen their shin muscles in order to comfortably walk athletically. By doing these exercises, you will reduce your chance of injury and enable yourself to walk faster.

This exercise is done by walking on your heels, taking short strides with your toes pointed as high as possible. Each stride should be no more than six inches. Walk this way for about 25 yards. If your shins tire quickly, stop walking on your heels briefly and stretch your shins a little. Then complete the exercise. If 25 yards is really easy, go a little farther.

Remember, it is not a race. You will gain more from doing this exercise slowly than quickly. It is a good idea to do the shin stretching exercises explained earlier after you complete this exercise.

CURB SHIN EXERCISE

Another exercise for the shins can be done on the edge of a curb.

Face away from the curb. Place your heels as close to the edge as you can while maintaining your balance. Start with your toes pointed down toward the ground.

Now move your toes up and down as quickly as you can. Each time you raise/lower your toes, they should be raised/lowered as high/low as possible.

Try to repeat this exercise 20 or 30 times.

FORWARD STRAIGHT LEG LIFT

All of these exercises can be done with or without a light ankle weight. Start without weight and then graduate to using light weights. Never use weights exceeding 10% of your body weight.

The first exercise is done by lying on your back and keeping one leg straight. The other leg should be raised to form a triangle with the ground.

Raise the straight leg to about 45 degrees, hold it there for a second, and lower it.

Repeat this 15 times for each leg.

SIDE STRAIGHT LEG LIFT

Lie on your side and keep both legs straight at your side.

Raise the top leg to about 45 degrees, hold it for a second, and then lower it back down again.

Repeat this 15 times for each leg.

MORE DIFFICULT STRAIGHT LEG LIFT

Lie on your right side and keep your right leg straight. Cross your left leg over your right. Place your left foot on the ground slightly above and perpendicular to your right knee.

Now raise your right leg a few inches off the ground. Hold it there for a second and lower it back.

Repeat this 15 times for each leg.

LEG EXTENSION

This exercise strengthens the quadriceps. If you have access to a gym, you can use a machine there, but ask someone how to do it. Many machines vary, so it would be best to get advice on the exact machine that you are using.

If however, you do this exercise at home, you can simulate the machine. You may try this on a high bar or kitchen stool. With an ankle weight or bag hung from your foot, sit as far back on the stool as you can.

Then, raise your foot and try to straighten your leg. Lower your leg and repeat it 15 times. Be careful not to lock the knee as the leg raises.

LEG CURL

The last leg exercise is for the hamstrings. This exercise is best done on a conventional leg curl machine; however, if you do not have access to one, you might try this. You can do this exercise without an ankle weight or with a light weight wrapped around your ankle.

Stand next to a wall and balance against it with your arms.

Slowly lift one leg to a little past 90 degrees. Then lower your leg to the beginning position.

Repeat this 15 times with each leg.

ARM SWING EXERCISE

The goal of this exercise is to simulate walking in place while holding a light weight in each hand. This exercise has many benefits. Not only can you work out your arms, improving your strength, flexibility, and technique, but you will increase the flexibility and improve the technique of your hips as well. However, to achieve all of these benefits, you must have mastered some of the basic athletic walking techniques explained within this book. If you have not learned them, come back to this exercise later.

The *Arm Swing Exercise* works best with light weights in each hand. Try not to use dumbbells, because you may accidentally hit your hips with them. Try to use flat plates instead. You should start with 1 to 2 lb. weights and build up to 10 to 15 lb. weights.

Allow your arms to swing back and forth as described in the walking technique chapter. Pay careful attention to keeping your shoulders relaxed and your arms in the proper range of motion. Allow your hips to rotate back and forth. The weights in your hands should help to drive your hips through a greater range of motion than you normally achieve while walking. Your legs should pivot back and forth allowing your knee to come forward and back. Finally, as your knee comes forward, make sure your heel is lifted off the ground.

*Right Leg
Forward*

Right Leg Back

MISCELLANEOUS TOPICS

INJURIES

We would all like to believe that our sport is injury free. However, the unfortunate reality is that although walkers have fewer injuries than other athletes, injuries may occur just as they do in any other aerobic sport where your body weight is on a single leg at a time.

Athletic walking is unique in that it demands a certain symmetry of motion. Each lower limb must perform similar functions. Otherwise, the alignment is thrown off. Just as potholes effect a car, lumps and bumps cause painful strains and inflammation of muscles and joints.

To assist in your recovery when injuries occur, you should follow these guidelines for treatment - but remember they are not a substitute for a **doctor's** opinion. As all the experts in the field will tell you, make sure you consult a primary care physician or other medical provider when your front line treatment does not work or when the problem worsens.

Causes

There are several different causes of injury. One of the most common is overuse and occurs for several important reasons.

1. A sudden large increase in mileage adds excessive stress to the leg joints. An injury is the body's response.
2. A continual increase in mileage, without allowance for the body to adapt. At first, the walker may feel that he did nothing different, but it is the training load that can have a cumulative effect.
3. A change in terrain to hills, or from a soft to hard surface, or visa versa, can be a setup for injury.
4. A walker may select improper shoes. Initially, a shoe may feel comfortable, but if it is not supportive enough as the shoe breaks down, so does the foot.
5. A walker may rapidly change his technique without allowing the body to adapt by incorporating proper stretching exercises.

Other walkers develop injuries because they are walking with improper technique. Fortunately, these problems can be corrected by proper planning, following the techniques in this book, and good coaching. Notice that the training schedules have easy and hard weeks. It is important for all athletes to allow the body time to recuperate.

Pay attention to the road and road surface when you walk. An accidental trip on a curb, or walking into a car, can put a dent into more than just your training schedule.

So something hurts

What happens when we don't follow directions? We get punished as we do in other aspects of our life when we break the rules. Once injured, it is important that we treat the injury properly. It is also important that we do not continue to abuse the injury by continuing to walk.

When injured, the first treatment is to reduce or stop walking until the injury has healed. Most people rationalize that they can train through an injury, because they don't want to get out of shape. It is important to treat all injuries with respect. Unless you are a very experienced walker, have a knowledgeable coach, or a doctor gives you approval; **don't** train through your injuries. By training through an injury, walkers will often prolong the injury and their reduced walking fitness level will leave them less fit than had they rested and recovered properly.

What is an injury?

Injuries fit into two categories: acute and chronic. Acute injuries occur all of a sudden. A football player suffering a broken rib from being head-butted is an example. Chronic injuries, more common in walkers, occur because of an accumulated stress on an area of the body. The same principles apply to both.

When you first hurt your body, you have damaged tissue, your blood vessels bleed, and the injured area swells. This swelling will slow the healing process.

Once injured, the goal is to prevent the damage from spreading and to prevent the rest of the body from compensating for that injury. For example, an ankle sprain causes you to limp and favor it. The other foot then receives more stress and can begin to develop symptoms as well.

RICE

Your front line treatment is a simply one. Follow the traditional **RICE (Rest, Ice, Compression, Elevation)** method. The first step in RICE is to stop the activity that caused the injury and **rest**. **Ice** is used for several reasons. It is a great pain killer, it reduces swelling by reducing blood flow to the injured area, and it slows the release of other chemicals that retard the healing process.

Use large, soft ice packs if you can get them. The large, soft variety allows the pack to sculpt to the body easier than a bag of ice. If you can't find them, use a
98

large plastic bag filled with ice and water. If you have sensitive skin, place a paper towel between the ice and your body.

When using an ice treatment, apply the ice for 20 minutes, then remove it for 20 minutes. Finally, apply the ice for an additional 20 minutes. You can repeat this sequence a couple of times a day. As you start to walk again, it is especially important to use ice to prevent the return of swelling and pain after exercising. Do not delay applying ice to your injury by standing around talking to your training partner.

Be aware that there are a number of ailments, like arthritis, that may indicate that ice treatment is not the best for you. Please consult a doctor before you try this treatment for the first time.

A second method to reduce swelling is to take an anti-inflammatory, such as ibuprofen, aspirin, or naproxen. Many people will say that they can deal with the pain, but a pain cycle is self-defeating. It slows the healing process and forces you to compensate for the injury, so that other parts of your body may begin to hurt. Please ask your doctor if it is OK for you to use this therapy approach. Make sure that you are not sensitive to anti-inflammatory medication.

One problem with using pain killers is that many walkers, upon feeling pain-free, decide to go back out and walk again. They compound the injury and are worse off than before. Therefore, don't walk while you are taking pain killers.

Sometimes the injured body part needs **compression** or immobilization. Ace wraps and taping are two of the best approaches to limit motion, add support, and allow you to resume function with limited risk of further injury. Sometimes, however, these methods do not work and you may require full immobilization in the form of a cast or no weight bearing using crutches.

Elevation always helps, but remember in order to keep the water (swelling) from running downhill, you must keep the injured body part at least to the level of your heart. Sometimes that means full bed rest.

When to use heat

Growing up, we were told to treat injuries with the trusty heating pad. While heat has its place in treatment, it can cause additional damage if it is applied too early. As a general rule of thumb, wait at least 48 hours from the onset of the injury for the swelling to stop. By heating the area, we increase the flow of blood and remove the waste products our body creates. To improve the effectiveness of applying heat, try to apply moist heat or alternate between heat and ice as your treatment.

Let the buyer beware

Do not be fooled by sports creams and ointments as a substitute for heat therapy. Most of these products are skin irritants, which gives the illusion of a heat treatment, but in reality simply heats the skin's surface.

Pain Problems

Many pain problems in the body can be treated with the RICE methodology. However, when a problem is chronic in nature, RICE is not enough. Along with RICE, we must add specific stretching exercises to enable the body part to resume normal function. Whether it is the lower back, heel, or any place in between, we must be aware of the type of problem and treat it specifically.

Muscle Strains

A muscle strain can occur in any of the major muscle groups. The treatment for each group is the same, RICE and lots of stretching.

Shin Splints

Shin splints occur when the balance in the lower leg muscles is disrupted, either by tightness or by weakness. Usually the weakness is in the muscles in the front of the leg. The pain is usually felt not in the muscle but in the shin, or tibia bone. The treatment for shin splints, in addition to RICE, is to stretch all the lower leg muscles. Include the following stretches in your recovery: *Traditional Calf Stretch*, *Bent Leg Calf Stretch,* and the *Shin Stretch.* To help prevent recurrence, make sure that you practice the exercise *Walking on Your Heels.*

Heel Pain

Heel pain can occur at the back of your heel, where the calf muscle attaches to the heel as the Achilles tendon. This pain can extend to the bottom of the heel and into the arch of the foot. The treatment for both types of injuries are the same, in addition to RICE, stretch the calf muscles using the *Traditional Calf Stretch* and the *Bent Leg Calf Stretch,* and try not to walk barefoot. Finally, adding a support to the arch and heel in the shoe may be helpful.

Common Injuries Not Treated By RICE

Skin problems

Certain skin infections enjoy the added heat and humidity of the athletic shoe environment, namely **warts and fungus.**

Athlete's Foot

Commonly known as "athlete's foot," a fungal infection of the foot usually begins with peeling skin and redness between the toes. It can cause itching and may also involve the nails after some time. While athlete's foot can be treated with over-the-counter powders, creams and solutions, be aware that it can recur. Keep the feet dry, throw your shoes in the washing machine with bleach (an enemy of fungus), and use socks that wick moisture away from the feet.

Warts

Plantar warts are small thickened growths that usually occur on the soles of the feet. They can be very painful if they are directly under the weight-bearing part of the foot. Caused by a viral organism, they can be treated by over-the-counter solutions. However, be aware that they can recur and spread. Do not be tempted to either shave or cut them off since you can spread them to yourself or others. Follow the directions for treatment carefully and keep the feet dry.

Blisters

One of the most common problems for beginning walkers, as well as more experienced walkers, is blisters. Friction caused by improperly fitting walking shoes, particularly if one of your feet is larger than the other, is an obvious culprit, but it's not the only one. Irregular walking terrain can also lead to blisters.

Everyone's question is to pop or not to pop the blister. It is recommend that you do **not** pop a blister: An open wound invites unwanted organisms. Depending on the size and location of a blister, usually a sterile covering will protect it and prevent more friction. A salt solution soak will help to shrink it, and an antiseptic such as iodine or alcohol will prevent infection. For recurring blisters, consider the source, which may involve a change in the way the foot contacts the ground in the shoe. Often, a change of the insoles of the shoe can make a difference in the amount of friction that occurs on the foot.

Nail problems

With constant pressure from improperly fitting shoes, blood vessels can break under the nail and cause blood to collect underneath, leading to a condition called **black toenail.** Usually, this does not cause pain, but may lead to the loss of your toenail. If pain exists, soaking the foot in warm water may release the blood underneath the nail and alleviate the pain. Obviously, professional medical attention should be sought in this case.

Thickening of the toenails, can also be related to constant pressure without a change in color. Fungus can enter into these nails, make them difficult to cut, and contribute to their loss and pain.

Height as well as width of the toebox of the shoe is usually the cause of these ailments. The shape of the toes or contracture of the joints can also play a significant role.

On the road again

When starting back on a training regimen, do not repeat the steps that caused the injury. First and foremost, start back slowly. You will be tempted to try to make up the time you have lost by training more, but you will re-injure yourself. A good rule of thumb is to give your body an additional two or three days from the time you feel healed before you start to walk. This will allow your body the time it requires to completely heal.

BASIC NUTRITION FACTS

To combat the nutritional fads that change with the times, one should subscribe to a basic nutritional philosophy-one without the hype and miracle results, but with a common sense approach that, combined with exercise, will lead to a healthy lifestyle. Before we discuss it, let's review some unfortunate nutritional facts.

The spot reduction myth

One of the least understood nutritional facts is: You can **not** spot reduce. Spot reduction is the idea that by working the muscles in the areas that you have excess fat, you can reduce the fat in those areas. A simple example is the belief that doing sit-ups will reduce the fat around your stomach. Doing sit-ups accomplishes many things. It strengthens the abdominal muscles, which in turn reduces the stress on your back. However, it does not significantly reduce the fat around your stomach.

While many people will swear they have techniques or approaches that work this way, it is simply untrue. The sad fact is that the first areas we put fat on are the last areas from which we take the fat off. Therefore, if we are trying to lose that last ten pounds around our hips, we may also have to lose the 20 pounds around our stomachs.

When the author was in high school, an overweight man came into the gym and, with all seriousness, wanted to know if he simply did ten sit-ups a day, would he be able to eat anything he wanted. The answer then was the same as the answer today: No.

A simple formula

Weight gain or loss follows and always has followed a seemingly simple formula. Everyone will fall into one of three categories:

- If the amount of calories consumed equals the amount of calories expended by your body, your weight is maintained.
- If you take in more calories than you consume, you will gain weight.
- If you take in fewer calories than you expend, you will lose weight.

It gets complex because all people do not burn the same number of calories participating in the same activities. When the author was in college, his professor wanted his students to count the calories they consumed and the calories they burned each day. They were to use a standard chart of calories burned per exercise to calculate their total expenditure for the day. The author explained that this method would not work for everyone, but the teacher disagreed and made the students count calories anyway. At the end of the week, his method dictated that the author should gain an average of more than two pounds per week! That would be 100 pounds a year. So by the teacher's calculation, the author should now weigh nearly 1,000 lbs. Needless to say, the author weighs slightly less than that. Why didn't the teacher's method work?

Varying metabolisms

The professor's method didn't account for the fact that everyone has different metabolisms. The author is blessed with a metabolism that is stuck in high gear all the time. This means that if he is simply sitting in a chair, he may be burning more calories than the person next to him. Society has considered this a blessing, but in reality the author's body is less efficient than someone who burns fewer calories per activity.

Because individuals' metabolisms vary, the author finds it of limited use to count calories. Instead, if the author is concerned about weight gain or loss (believe it or not, it can be just as difficult to gain weight as it is to lose it), he concerns himself with a relative change in diet. But diet alone is not enough. It is important to realize that neither exercising nor dieting alone will make a huge difference.

A combined effort is needed

If a person tries to lose weight only by dieting, the body senses that it is not receiving enough food and slows down the metabolism. Therefore, fewer calories are burned per activity than if one had not dieted at all. This makes the diet self-defeating.

But, if a person increases his or her exercise and the amount of food he intakes in, no real weight loss will occur. By increasing exercise without overly increasing caloric intake, you stand the best chance for success. If you increase the amount you exercise, you not only burn calories while exercising, but also increase your metabolism for hours afterward. To maximize the benefit from exercise, make sure you do not exercise and then go to sleep. The benefit of your increased metabolism from walking will be lost.

Additionally, when you exercise, you build more muscle. The simple presence of more muscle in the body leads to an increase in metabolism. This increase in metabolism is another factor that makes counting calories difficult.

Is all weight loss good?

The goal of weight loss is to lose fat, not muscle. A good measure of the effectiveness of a dieting and exercise program is to measure percent body fat instead of measuring absolute weight.

A person's body fat can be measured in a number of ways. The most common are:

1. Skin calipers, which measure the amount of fat around arms, legs, waist, etc.
2. An electronic device.
3. A water submersion tank.

The first two methods are the most common and are usually accurate within 2%.

While elite male athletes may have body fat as low as 3% to 5%, a healthy male may have approximately 15% to 18%. Similarly an elite woman's body fat is about 10% to 15%, while the normal healthy rating is about 20% to 25%.

How about a late-night snack?

When you go to sleep, your metabolism slows down. If you eat a meal before going to sleep, your body does not have a chance to burn off the calories it has consumed. Therefore, by eating late at night, more calories may end up stored as fat.

Is a calorie a calorie?

All men/women may be created equal, but not all calories are. Aside from the health benefits/risks of maintaining the proper levels of fat in your diet, eating a calorie of fat as opposed to a calorie of a complex carbohydrate will not yield the same results. Eating carbohydrates and then exercising promotes the use of those calories. Eating fat allows the calories to be stored as fat easier.

How much fat is enough? Different experts quote different amounts. A baseline rule of thumb is that no more than 20% to 30% of your calories should come from fat. Fortunately, it is relatively easy to count the fat in your diet. Labels for processed foods now contain not only the amount of fat, but also the percentage of calories from fat contained in a product. Be careful, you may think you are eating something low in fat because it says "reduced fat," "25% less fat than regular," etc., but these may not be as low as desired. You might think that products like turkey burgers are low in fat; but if they are made with all dark meat, they are really quite high in fat. Labels can be very deceiving. A can of "healthy" soup was labeled 99% fat-free while more than 25% of its calories still came from fat.

The author follows a simple rule of thumb. He tries to eat most staple foods that are lower than 30% (preferably 20%) in fat. Salads (with small amounts of low or no fat dressing), white meat chicken without the skin, fish, rice, vegetables, and pasta are all regulars on his dinner plate. Then, if he is going to snack, he tries to have most of his snacks contain about 30% of the calories from fat. This way he does not have to total calories and drive himself into a neurotic frenzy. Also, by keeping a reasonable eye on fat intake, he does not feel guilty when he reaches for the ice cream. Remember his earlier golden rule, "If you want a cookie, have a cookie, just don't have the whole bag of cookies." Unless your doctor has told you to restrict fat intake severely, don't try to achieve a no-fat diet. Remember, if the low-fat food has any taste to it, it is highly probable that the fat is replaced with another evil, most commonly sugar or sodium. Although studies have not shown it yet, it does not take much of an imagination to conclude that there are going to be negative effects from all the sugar people are consuming as a substitute to fat.

Beware of the hype

Many products out there claim to be the answer to all your exercise blues. The author recently attended a product seminar on *healthful* products. The distributor made all sorts of claims about each product. This one will cause you to have more energy, while that one will cause fat to miraculously leave your system. While some of these products can be extremely helpful, how can you determine the knowledgeable, honest salesman from the one selling snake oil?

By asking the following questions of salespeople, you may be able to tell how authentic their claims are:

1. If the salesman states that a medical study proved something, ask how many people were in the study. Then ask to see the study. The author was assured at a seminar that there were a lot of people in the study. When he read the study, it turned out to be only a little over 20. 20 people are not enough to prove results beyond a reasonable statistical doubt.
2. If the salesman states that his product is better than another and then shows statistics, ask about other statistics that are not shown. At a seminar the author attended, the salesman claimed his sports drink was better than the one the author was using. The salesman claimed this because his had more electrolytes than the author's brand. The author asked what other ingredients were contained in the drink mix? The author's had a glucose polymer that is

supposed to give the athlete more energy than regular fructose. The salesman had no idea what he was talking about.

3. Be aware of any claims stated something like, "I'm not allowed to tell you this, but this product has been found to lower blood pressure, reduce cholesterol, etc.." Ask the salesman why he is not allowed to claim it. Salesmen often try to play off your emotions. If the FDA has not approved the product for certain purposes, don't believe the salesman.

4. Also be aware of how the product is marketed. If it is marketed using a network marketing technique, be very cautious. Usually, these companies are merely pyramid structures in which profit is made by building a distributor network. These companies are often more concerned with their downline (the size of their network) than how many products they sell. That's why you don't see advertisements for their products in newspapers, magazines, TV, or even the Internet. Ask why they are not marketing it through traditional channels.

Many of these salespeople are not necessarily dishonest, they have merely been taken in by the lure of easy money and a desire to believe in these products.

The pre-race meal

When it comes to preparing for a race, eat a nice, healthful portion of pasta the night before the race. Make sure that you do not have a cream sauce, because it is high in fat and hard to digest. Also, it is usually safer to stay away from spicy sauces as well. Many beginning walkers think that they need to carbo-load before a race. We do not recommend that walkers preparing for a short race or even first-time marathoners or recreational racers carbo-load. Carbo-loading is quite different from simply eating lots of pasta and bread the night before a big race. Carbo-loading consists of depleting the body of carbohydrates, eating protein in the days before the marathon, and finally eating large amounts of pasta in an attempt to trick your body into storing more energy in your muscles. This process can be stressful to your body and should be avoided by all but the most serious athletes.

MENTAL PREPARATION

It was 4:00 a.m. on the day of the author's first international competition. You would expect that he would be sound asleep, resting for his race. Instead, to put it as politely as possible, he was bent over a toilet "tossing his cookies."

At the time, he thought he must have eaten something that disagreed with his stomach. In reality, although he had trained hard and was focused on the race, he had not prepared himself completely for the competition. He left out one key element, mental training. It was stress that led to his early morning trip to the bathroom, and it could have been avoided. By learning simple visualization techniques, pre-race stress can be reduced or eliminated.

Your first race

When recreational walkers decide to enter a race, they may suffer from some of the same problems that the author did in Canada. Many walkers pay careful attention to a training schedule like the ones provided in this book. Often people boast how they follow them religiously. They make sure that they get in the exact mileage, rain or shine.

Unfortunately, by focusing so closely on a schedule, walkers leave out the other important aspects of training. One of these is stretching. Despite constant warnings, walkers often reduce/eliminate their stretching in order to complete the scheduled miles. Another training component that walkers leave out is something that they may not even be aware that they can do something about. This activity is exercising the mind. While it does not build any actual muscles, it can be a vital part of a good race.

Exercising the mind

It is important to be prepared not just physically, but mentally as well. Many walkers express concerns about what the race course will be like. Who will be there? When is the post-race party? Many of these questions can be answered, thereby relieving some anxiety, but others cannot. Instead of letting fear fester, learn to visualize what can happen and how to deal with it. No one can tell you exactly what will happen at a given time, so you need to prepare yourself for all possibilities. Proper preparation can reduce the anxiety that builds up.

How can you prepare your mind so that you are more relaxed the day of the race? By exercising your mind along with the body. By using self-hypnosis, you can teach yourself to be more relaxed on race day.

How to do it

Self-hypnosis is not accomplished by waving a watch in front of your eyes, nor will you bark like a dog when you are through. Self-hypnosis, like regular hypnosis, is just a form of relaxation. By learning to relax, you allow your mind to be more susceptible to suggestion. Once relaxed, you can plant positive suggestions about the race and have them stay there.

Let's relax

The best way to learn to relax is to use mental imagery. Start by finding a place where you can lie down undisturbed. Assume a comfortable position. (You can make an audio tape of this lesson, or tell yourself the steps in your mind. When the author started these techniques, the co-author talked him through it. Later, the author used a tape to mimic what the co-author was saying. Finally, a tape was no longer necessary, because it was possible for the author to simply think about the steps.)

Once in a relaxed position, imagine yourself in a quiet, relaxed setting, maybe on the beach or near a lake. Imagine a fire is by your feet, warming them. Then begin a slow process of imaging the warmth from the fire traveling up your feet, through your legs and into your upper body. Then, allow the warmth to travel to your arms and head. Once you're relaxed, imagine your body getting light, and then heavy, and then light again. By this point, you should be very relaxed. Start to repeat positive suggestions about your race.

It is best to have a script for the upcoming race. Concentrate on the steps needed to succeed in reaching your goal, not the goal itself. Therefore, start by imagining what race day will be like. Try not to get specific about factors you can't control, like the weather, but center on things like:

- Imagine being relaxed and confident that you can accomplish your goal.
- Imagine seeing your training partners showing up.
- Imagine the race starting and feeling good, because you have trained hard and well.
- Imagine passing the mile markers of the race, happy at your pace and comfort level.

At this point, repeat many of the positive suggestions that you use during your training sessions. By repeating to yourself all the suggestions about how to improve your walking stride, you will automatically remember the suggestions during the race. It will be like having your own private coach inside your head.

Make sure you imagine everything the way you want it to happen all the way through the finish line.

The key to the success of this method is remaining in a relaxed state throughout the exercise. If you are making a tape to listen to, make sure that you speak in a monotone voice throughout the session.

STARTING YOUR OWN CLUB

In other sports, there may be a great deal of camaraderie, but it is usually after the game. Walking allows for camaraderie before, during, and after, especially if you are a member of a supportive walking club. But where can one find a good walking club?

A club can be an important part of a person's walking program. Clubs offer camaraderie, information, coaching, and events. Some areas, like New York City, are blessed with many clubs. It is important to pick a club that meets your needs. Some clubs are geared strictly for the elite race walkers, while others are for recreational walkers. Some clubs, like ours, are a mixture of both. In one race, the author was pushing really hard and won, but was exhausted. Ten minutes later, one of his walkers strolled across the finish line and commented, "Did you see the wonderful sunset?" At the time, the author didn't even know the sun went down. He enjoyed his race, and so did his walker, but they enjoyed it for different reasons.

The author's club is called the Philadelphia Area Striding Team, or PHAST. Instead of centering on strict competitiveness, PHAST revolves around having a good time while walking. Therefore, the walkers do not pick their competitions by the level of the competition alone, but what other niceties they might find along the way. For this reason they go to a race up by Niagara Falls and another by the Washington Monument in D.C. This way, there is a little something for everyone, including the spectators who travel with the racers to the competition.

Unfortunately, not everyone lives in a community with an active walking program that meets his/her needs. When the author arrived in Philadelphia in 1985, race walking and formal walking programs were virtually non-existent. There might have been a few token races, but no organized clinics or training sessions. The author believes he could count the number of race walkers he saw in five years on his fingers.

In 1989, the author suffered a knee injury and decided to use his rehabilitating time to organize a club. The method he followed is one that you can follow, with one exception. He had already found a coach: himself. If you are interested in finding a coach, go to the section *Organizations*, on page 125. It is an excellent place to begin your search.

The First Step

Start by finding a few people interested in learning about walking. The most knowledgeable person should start to coach them and hold formal clinics. This is what the author did.

If none of your peers knows enough about walking, after you finish reading this book, attend a race walking clinic and become the coach yourself. At the time the author started PHAST, he was a poor college student, so he charged a fee for his lessons, but this is optional. (Believe it or not, people respond better when you charge, because they believe they are getting something for their money. They are also more apt to come each week if they've paid for it.)

How to Find More People

The first few members in PHAST found a couple more, and suddenly PHAST became a nice little group. At that point, PHAST formed an official USA Track & Field club (see page 125), and they were off and walking, literally. Although there was a very light and carefree attitude in the club, they did do one business-like function that has paid off time and time again. They printed business cards that had the names and numbers of the key people in the area that someone could call for information on the club. Business cards are easy to carry, inexpensive to print, and easy to distribute when you are out walking. It is when you are out walking that you will most likely meet prospective club members. You simply need to speak up and let people know there is a club. How many times have you met someone while working out and wished you had a pen? The business cards will solve that problem.

PHAST also used the cards when they participated in local running/walking races. After the author finished he would sit at the finish line and hand cards to all the walkers who came in after him. After each race, PHAST would gain a few more participants.

Eventually, clubs grow and it is difficult for one person to do everything, so don't. The single biggest advice we can give you is to empower individuals in your club to help. One person can be in charge of the newsletters, another collecting money and keeping a club registry, another is the coach, and so on.

It is important to realize that it is everyone's club, and by empowering people, let them make the decisions, even if you don't agree. You may wish to reserve veto power, but use it sparingly.

How much should your club charge?

How much your club should charge for membership is really up to you. PHAST usually charges $15/person per year. However, last year they had so much money left over, they decided not to charge anyone for the year. PHAST runs the club more like a family than anything else. PHAST no longer actively recruits; people find it. The members of PHAST are glad to train them and if they want, they join. The author thinks a large club leads to politics and personality conflicts, and he personally doesn't care how many people are in it. The author believes he has around 40-50 members, of which 20+ are active, but he leaves the tracking of such numbers to other members of the club.

You can charge separately for membership and clinics. You may give a T-shirt with your membership or sell shirts, sweats, etc. separately. It really depends how much money you think your club needs. PHAST decided that the club was not going to sponsor individuals to go to races. The author thought this would create bitterness within the club and just lead to problems. Instead, PHAST members share expenses and travel together.

EXCUSES, JUSTIFICATIONS, AND FURTHER EXCUSES

Have you had something important to do and pondered skipping your workout? Did you want to eat something fattening? Have you had a bad race with no reason? While it is a bad habit to consistently skip workouts and gain 100 lbs., occasionally breaking your schedule when life gets in the way is OK. So that you do not stress out over diversion, the author, being a benevolent dictator of a coach, has provided you with a series of excuses that must be true, because after all, the coach said so.

Missed workouts

- I'm tapering for the big race.
- I'm tapering for the big workout.
- Well, the miles I drive my car count.
- The weather isn't nice, and I wouldn't want to get sick.
- I need a new pair of shoes, wearing the old ones may risk injury.
- I'm making sure that I don't hurt myself.
- If I don't get my work done, I'll be fired and then I'll have no money to train.
- My partner couldn't walk, so I didn't, so he wouldn't feel guilty.
- I just didn't want to do it.
- My dog ate my training schedule.
- I need to watch the Pittsburgh Steelers' playoff game.
- It's icy out, and I wouldn't want to get hurt.

Fattening foods

- I need the extra calories for my long walk.
- Your body needs a certain amount of fat every day.
- ... but, it's a low-fat hot fudge sundae with heaping gobs of whipped cream and mounds of ice cream.
- There are no calories, because I am eating it in a sports mug.
- There are no calories, because I am thinking thin.
- **There are no calories in any of the food that I eat while taking the coach out to eat.**
- I'm carbo-loading for the big race.
- I deserve this because of the 20-miler I walked today.
- I deserve this, because of the 20-miler I will walk tomorrow.
- This is special food that I cannot normally get where I live, e.g. New York pizza.

A bad race

- It was my coach's fault.
- I didn't have my lucky sneakers.
- My coach poisoned me with his cooking the night before.
- It was too hot.
- It was too cold.
- It was too windy.
- The course was much more hilly than they said it would be.
- You weren't there to cheer me on.
- It was too nice outside.
- This really cute girl/guy was watching, and it distracted me.
- I'm not concerned about time, because that is for the egomaniacs.
- I have been sick all week.
- I have had too much to do at work.
- The scag player I hired to walk for me did not show up.

Stretching

- There are no excuses not to stretch; always stretch before and after a workout (sorry!).

BIOGRAPHIES

Walking is a sport of all ages, fitness levels, and athletic ambitions. The traditional approach to a sports book is to have elite athletes' biographies listed. However, many people cannot directly relate to the motivation of elite athletes. Instead, we have included the full spectrum of athletic walkers from our clubs. This includes: recreational walkers, somewhat competitive walkers, and walkers who are considered elite in their age groups. In contrast to elite athletes, whose training starts early, these athletes came from varying athletic backgrounds. Some did not participate in sports when they were younger, while others participated only when young and not again for almost half a century. The similarities and differences in their stories brings encouragement to those who have not started and a connection to those who have been walking for years, but didn't know the motivation and history behind anyone's beginnings.

Thomas Zdrojewski

Thomas Zdrojewski, known as Tommy Z, grew up in the late '50s in the suburbs of a mid-size Eastern city. He was living the script for *American Graffiti*, school, hot-rods, girls, rock & roll music, and of course the Friday night football game. He did not play organized sports, opting to channel his talents to playing the trumpet. These efforts paid dividends and he was accepted to both the Juilliard School of Music and the Navy's Music School.

Choosing neither one, Thomas chose instead to marry, raise two daughters, and work in the construction field as a mechanic. During this time, he played organized semi-professional football. He competed on an organized softball team, which eventually became 2-time state champions.

Through the years, his profession took him to the ranks of management, and a sometime desk job where life became less physically demanding. Like many of us, he found his once-fit body *ballooning*, and he gained 60 pounds. Realizing one morning that the simple act of tying his shoes had to be thought out in advance, he enlisted his neighbor's help, and together they started walking through the neighborhood hoping to shed some of their *unwanted baggage*.

After only partly fulfilling his goals, he found himself entering a local 5K run/walk race. This eventually led to Tommy Z meeting the author. Because of this chance meeting, they became coach/student and friends.

For the last six years, through the author's tutelage, Tommy Z has realized many goals within the race walking community, except perhaps getting anyone

116

to be able to pronounce his last name. He has received numerous local and national awards, the most prestigious of which is the national age group championship in the very grueling 40K event (almost 25 miles), which he won three times, placing sixth overall in 1994.

Through dedication, hard work, and much support from his family, friends, and peers, Tommy Z has realized more than he could have hoped for, including losing the 60 pounds.

Jack Starr

Looking at national age group record holder Jack Starr, you would never guess that he has not been race walking his whole life. Jack grew up during the Great Depression, when there was no time for playing sports. He developed a strong work ethic and learned to set goals: save up for a bike; get an after-school job; save money; get better grades; win a college scholarship. He worked during college, got drafted, and when he came out of the Army went back to college while he was working. Instead of taking it easy, Jack had a series of demanding jobs with DuPont, a great young family, and the obligations of both. There were lots of goals to strive for, but, in his mind at least, more important things to spend his time on than sports.

Although Jack did not participate, he was a great fan of every sport. In the late '60s, he was really intrigued by stories about a fellow DuPonter trying to qualify for the Olympics by training for some "goofy sport." The sport was race walking, of course, and the man was Dave Romansky.

Many years later, when Jack was able to retire, he finally convinced himself that it was OK to spend time "playing." He looked for a sport that he could really enjoy. None of the usual pastimes like golf, etc., seemed right, but race walking did. So he started walking in his neighborhood, until he got up the courage to enter a local 5K meet. In September 1992 he entered his first race, and he loved it! In a few months he improved enough to win some races and realize he was faster than most walkers half his age.

In a strange twist of fate, he happened to see Dave Romansky at a local meet. He introduced himself, and perhaps because Jack told Dave how he had enjoyed reading about him years ago, Dave invited Jack and some others for a workout. Dave told Jack he was a "tough old coot" (which thrilled Jack), and told Jack whom he had to beat to get national recognition.

At another local meet, Jack met PHAST members Tommy Z and Ed Gawinski. Tom invited Jack to join the club, and it was a great move! PHAST is a club where race walking is a priority, but having fun, making friendships, and supporting one another are just as important.

Jack has had some great races all over the **world** and has been competitive in every race he has entered. In May 1994, after training hard under the author's coaching, and with great race day encouragement from Tommy Z, he won his age group at the USATF 10K national championship and set a new national age group record. Although he lost most of the winter and spring to a hamstring problem, he managed to defend that championship in 1995. When he doesn't win a race, he's never overjoyed, but because the race walking community so supportive, he still gives sincere congratulations to those who finish ahead of him.

Jack still enjoys setting goals for himself and pursues them actively. In 1996, his goals were to repeat as national 10K champion and place in the WAVA 30K race walk in Brugge, Belgium. He reached both.

Jack credits his race walking program for keeping him fit; He feels better than he did ten years ago, and each day brings a new challenge.

Ed Merrill

Ed Merrill was born and raised in Wilmington, Del., where he attended Catholic grade and high school. During his high school years, he played JV football, but because he weighed only 125 lbs., he was never a threat to become an All-American. During his junior year, Ed did achieve a certain amount of notoriety and made the varsity track team as a sprinter.

After graduating from high school in 1950, he joined the Navy and spent the next four years on a destroyer traveling throughout the world. His 4-year hitch included two around the world cruises, two crossings of the equator, numerous trips to the Caribbean, two tours of duty in Korea.

When he was discharged from the Navy in 1955, he loafed around a bit until he was hired by the Diamond State Telephone Company and spent the next 30 years installing and repairing telephones. He really enjoyed working for Diamond State, but in 1986 he'd decided that he had enough and retired.

Like many high school athletes, in the years between his high school days and his retirement, his association with any activity that could be described as athletic was non-existent, and his body showed it. In 1950, he was 5' 8" and 120-125 lbs. In 1986, he was still 5' 8" and a 193 lb. munchkin. He kept telling himself that he had to lose weight and get in shape, but like most overweight people, he never got around to actually doing anything about it.

The straw that finally broke the elephant's back came from his young granddaughter, who after seeing his bulging beer belly, asked her mother when Pop-Pop was going to have his baby. Well, that did it!

Almost immediately, he started walking. Because he wasn't in very good physical shape -- actually terrible physical shape -- he started easy. He walked only a mile a day for several weeks. He slowly increased his mileage and pace and within a few months, was walking five miles a day at what Ed felt was a good pace. But best of all, Ed started to lose weight. After one year, Ed had lost an amazing 43 lbs. and felt great.

During one of his walks through a local park, Ed pondered entering a local running/walking race. He finally got up the courage and entered a 5K race. It was quite a shock to Ed. There were more than 400 runners and walkers. He felt like backing out and becoming a spectator, but he decided that since he was there he might as well enter. What an experience he had. Although he didn't finish first, he didn't finish last, either. He didn't meet any of the race walkers in the race, because they were too far ahead. But at the next race, he met the author and some of the other clubs members from the PHAST race walking club.

That race was over six years ago and he has been training with the club ever since. He describes the members of the club as not just his teammates, but as his family. Together they have traveled throughout the county, competing and socializing with other walkers from around the world.

During his last six years, he has met and competed with race walkers of all levels from world-ranked elite Olympic race walkers to top ranked masters walkers to novice walkers.

Ceane Rabada

When Ceane Rabada turned 40 over five years ago, she realized that her maintenance-free body days were over. As luck would have it, the adult school catalog arrived. Page 46 listed race walking.

> Do you like the outdoors, it asked? Ceane said yes.
> Do you like to walk? Love to.
> Would you like to increase your aerobic exercise? Sure.
> Would you like to meet others who share your interest? Yep!

Try race walking, it advised. So Ceane did. She has been enjoying all the above and more.

The class she attended helped to start the author's club, PHAST, The Philadelphia Area Striding Team. Ceane's question was, why aren't we called the Philadelphia Area Race Walking Team (PHART)? Hint, its not just because we wanted to include all forms of walking.

Ceane realizes that some team members are a whole lot "phaster" than others, but she says that every train needs a caboose. That has been her role on the team. Having never won a race, what prizes does the caboose take home? They aren't made of gold, silver, or bronze, but...

- Good friends that only come from sharing a passion.
- Personal achievement beyond personal expectation.
- **Friendly** competition.
- Lots of laughs.
- The beauty of nature in every season (Yes, even winter!).

The "prizes" are as numerous as the footsteps. So where's the gold for the not-so-fast walkers? It's in the sunset. While the 8-minute and 9-minute milers fly by her on their way to pick up their first place medal, her prize is the gorgeous golden sunset that a 13-minute mile pace allows her to take in, in all of its beauty. She can remember it on command.

Athletic walking at any pace is an affirmation of the saying that it is not the destination but the journey. It's in the "showing up", in "being on the court" instead of in the stands. In being out there, she has learned that there's a place for everyone in walking. She has found a lifelong friend that promises a long life.

Karen Rush-Monroe

Karen is no stranger to the benefits of sports, having participated in hiking, running, and rowing. She has discovered many of the overall health benefits associated with participating in an exercise program: fewer colds, stress relief, weight maintenance, etc. Karen will vouch that race walking achieves all this with a newly found strength and flexibility, but her love affair with race walking did not happen overnight. When she first started to race walk, she had neither flexibility or coordination. The author affectionately dubbed her the *poster child* of the team. She watched others glide around the track but had difficulty translating the hip-swinging motion into anything other than an awkward, stiff-legged walk. She persisted because the group was fun; while competitive, the others never made her feel out of place or too slow. Bit by bit, the whole arm, hip, and leg motion fell into place, and when it did, she finally understood the grace and speed that can be accomplished through race walking.

For Karen, what gives race walking its edge over other sports has less to do with its current health benefits and more to do with its accessibility and long-term benefits. As a full-time public relations professional, her days are spent on the phone and her work week often exceeds 60 hours. What better sport than one that requires nothing more than a pair of good athletic shoes?

For Karen, the choice of a sport that fits her lifestyle is paramount. If it isn't easy or fun, the sport becomes a choice, workouts occur sporadically, and any real health benefits are limited. Race walking adapts to her schedule, and unlike team sports, can be done at the spur of the moment. On days when she has reached her quota of interacting with people, she can work out alone. While she enjoys the solitude race walking can provide, she also enjoys being part of a group effort and participating in racing as part of a team. She knows her race walking buddies are there when she needs them, as she is there for them when they need her.

But in addition to the ease in which race walking fits into her life, she continues with this sport for an even more important reason. As a women in her mid-30s who works in the health field, she knows that staying active will help her stay healthier as she ages. She wants to hike up mountains, take long walks, and travel as long as she can. She does not foresee a time when race walking will not be a part of her life. In the few races in which she has competed, it has been both disappointing and inspiring to her that she has been beaten by women a decade older than herself. She takes similar encouragement that she can't keep up with some of the older members of her club who surpass her by more than a generation. She finds it encouraging to attend a national race and find herself among the younger competitors. She

121

looks around the awards ceremonies to see vibrant, fit people whose ages stretch into the 80s and thinks this is where she wants to be and realizes that race walking will help her get there. Karen takes great pleasure in discovering a sport that not only works for her now, but will also work for her in the future.

Beth Yanci

Beth Yanci describes herself as a "walker" in the making. January 1996 was a time for Beth Yanci to set realistic goals. Unlike in the past, she set her goals not by the year, but in realistic amounts of time for each particular goal. Unrealistic goals had always waylaid her ability to achieve the set goals. Her 1996 goals were simple:

- become more physically active.
- begin to lose weight in a sensible fashion, so she could keep it off permanently.

Luckily for Beth, she became associated with the Leukemia Society of America (LSOA). LSOA had a wonderful opportunity. It would help train her to walk a marathon, 26.2 miles. It was a daunting task for a non-athlete. The LSOA would provide a walking coach (the author), provide training sessions, organize the travel (to Anchorage), and provide lots of encouragement. In exchange Beth was asked to obtain sponsors.

During the 16 weeks of the program, Beth was able to complete the marathon in 6 ½ hours and did so without any injuries. Although she has never been the type of individual to sustain weight loss, during the 16 weeks of training she lost 23 pounds, which is $1/3^{rd}$ of the total weight Beth wants to lose. Though the marathon is now over, she has continued to walk. She has joined a local race walking club and is still losing weight in a consistent pattern. She continues to head toward the completion of the goals she set for herself and is setting new goals that she would never have considered possible to accomplish just six months ago.

What Beth does not realize is that we are all walkers in training. Walking is an activity in which we constantly set new goals, with the only limit of achievement set by our minds.

ORGANIZATIONS

Some areas of the country are incredibly gorgeous, with huge tracts of open land and a low cost of living. The people who live there don't want you to know about their piece of heaven. They fear it will become overcrowded. On the other hand, most walkers are usually more than glad to share their knowledge. Sadly, they seldom have a mechanism to do so. One of the goals of this book is to disseminate not just knowledge of how to walk like an athlete, but also how to seek out further assistance and information. Therefore, we have provided background and contact information for some of the most helpful organizations involved in the promotion and organization of walking activities.

North American Race Walking Foundation (NARF)

The North American Race Walking Foundation was founded in 1986 by Elaine Ward and John MacLachlan to promote race walking primarily in the United States and Canada. The Foundation offers a variety of services to help walkers become involved in fitness and competitive race walking. These services include providing information on race walking clubs and coaches throughout the country; providing a general list of books and videos on technique, training, and racing; and providing information on judging and starting clubs.

In response to the perceived need of walkers who live outside the centers of race walking activity, the Foundation offers a video coaching service and personal training schedules. A membership program in the Foundation was started in 1993 to offer walkers priority service and immediate support in finding solutions to problems or answering questions related to race walking. Membership details will be sent on request.

For more information, call or fax (818) 577-2264 or write to the North American Race Walking Foundation (NARF), PO Box 50312, Pasadena Calif. 91115-0312. E-mail address: NARWF@aol.com

Walkers Club of America

One of, if not the oldest, active walking club in the United States is the Walkers Club of America. Established in 1911 by a group of competitive walkers, it promotes the sport of walking and encourages walking for competition and exercise. Through the years their most famous race was the Coney Island race walk, currently in its 86th year. It was so popular that race walking in the New York area was even nicknamed the Coney Island Walk.

The club offers:

- Assistance starting your own club.
- Quarterly newsletters.
- Instructor certification.
- Walking/vacation camps throughout the US.

For more information send a self addressed stamped envelope to:

Walkers Club of America
33 Saddle Lane
Levittown, NY 11756

Leukemia Society of America's Team in Training Program

Have you ever dreamed of walking a marathon? Have you thought it an impossible task? Have you come up with countless reasons not to try? The Team in Training Program, sponsored by the Leukemia Society of America, can make your dream a reality. The author has been coaching the walkers for the Eastern Pennsylvania Chapter for over a year, and it has been an incredibly rewarding experience.

Team In Training is a marathon training program in which novice and seasoned runners and walkers are trained to complete marathons. Since each walker on the Team has a different goal and athletic background, experienced walking coaches are available to tailor a training program which will enable you to reach your goal. You'll receive sound advice on technique, race strategies, equipment, injury prevention and nutrition. Your custom training program will improve your strength, flexibility, cardiovascular endurance and weight control.

Walkers will be further motivated knowing that their efforts help the Leukemia Society of America find a cure for leukemia, lymphoma, multiple myeloma and Hodgkin's disease.

Participants are asked to raise funds for the Leukemia Society through individual pledges and corporate sponsorships. The money is applied to research, patient aid, and community service programs of the Society. Last year, 6,000 Team In Training participants raised more than $9 million. One in every 47 people who ran or walked a marathon last year did so as a member of Team in Training.

For more information call, (800) 482-TEAM.

United States Track & Field (USATF)

For those walkers interested in competing, USATF is an important organization to become associated with. It is the national governing body for track and field, long distance running, race walking and cross country – and is the United States' member of the International Amateur Athletic Federation, the world governing body for Athletics.

Through its nationwide membership of more than 2,500 clubs, schools, colleges and universities, and other organizations interested in track and field, long distance running, and race walking, USATF promotes programs of training and competition for men and women and boys and girls of all ages; protects the interests and eligibility of its some 100,000 member-athletes; and establishes and maintains the sport's rules of competition.

In order to compete in many USATF meets, you must become a member. Fees vary, but currently average around $15/year for an athlete.

The national office can be contacted at:
USA Track & Field
One RCA Dome, Suite 140
Indianapolis, Indiana 46225
(317) 261-0500

http://www.wellnesscenter.com

The WellnessCenter is not your traditional organization. It is one of a growing number of virtual organizations housed on the Internet. The WellnessCenter, is owned and operated by the author and is like no other Web site. Funded through corporate sponsorships, the WellnessCenter houses an abundance of free wellness information ranging from walking, exercise, and anti-aging practices.

Utilizing the World Wide Web's interactive medium, users gain access to information about sponsors and storefronts with a click of the mouse or by using any number of powerful internal search engines. They have access to more information than would be available through traditional media.

The WellnessCenter Offers...

- Walking Wellness On-Line, the first truly interactive walking book on the Web. The origins of this book can be traced back to this site.
- USATF's National Race Walker, a newsletter reporting the official business of the US Track & Field's Race Walk Committee.
- Contact information for walking clubs, key individuals, and clinics.
- Listings of upcoming races and race results.
- The Wellness Galleria, an electronic Super-Mall containing a broad range of wellness products and services.
- EverYoung, a Free monthly anti-aging newsletter.
- And much, much more.

The WellnessCenter can also be reached using **http://www.racewalk.com**.

REFERENCES

Bricklin, Mark, *Walking for Health*, Rodale Press, Emmaus, PA, 1992

Costill, David. *Inside Running: Basics of Sports Physiology*. Benchmark Press, Indianapolis, 1986.

Gray, John, *Racewalking for Fun and Fitness*, Englewood Cliffs, NJ 1985

Hopkins, Julian *"Walks" in Athletes In Action: The Official IAAF Book on Track & Field Techniques*, (Howard Payne, ed.) Pelham Books, London 1985

Meyers, Casey, *Aerobic Walking,* Vintage, Prentice Hall, New York, 1987

Perry, Jacquelin. *Gait Analysis: Normal and Pathological Function, Slack, Thorofare*, NJ, 1992

Rudow, Martin, *Advanced Race Walking*, Technique Publications, Seattle, WA, 1987

Sweazey, Glenn, "Two Hundred Years of Competitive Walking," Unpublished, Toronto, Canada, 1981

Westerfield, Gary, "The Race Walk Coach," Vol I-III, Unpublished, Smithtown, NY 1987-1989

Westerfield, Gary. "Feel The Need For Speed?" The Walking Magazine, June/July, 1987

About the Authors

Jeff Salvage

One time international competitor, Jeff Salvage uses his knowledge of the sport of race walking to enhance the exercise programs of walkers of all backgrounds. From beginning health walkers to Olympic hopefuls, Jeff coaches walkers through the club he founded, Philadelphia Area Striding Team, and the Leukemia Society of America's Team in Training Program.

Jeff is also the USATF (United States Track & Field) Mid-Atlantic Race Walking Chairman; Director of the Walks at the Penn Relays; a college professor at Drexel University; and creator of the WellnessCenter (www.wellnesscenter.com), one of the largest Internet publishing centers for walking, health, and fitness information.

Gary Westerfield

A coach who was always interested in the science behind walking, Gary has written and lectured about walking for over twenty years. Currently, Gary coaches high school track & field athletes as well as some of the top junior race walkers in the country. He is also an IAAF (International Amateur Athletic Association) judge. Last year, Gary was honored for his dedication to the sport of race walking and received the USATF Life Time Contribution Award.

Gary has fulfilled many roles in race walking. At one time he was: an international competitor; coach to the United States Women's Race Walking Team; coordinator of the United States Men's & Women's race walking team; coach of the cross country, track, & race walking teams at the State University of New York, Stony Brook; Editorial Advisor to Prevention Magazine; and spokesperson for Natural Sport, a division of the Brown Shoe Company.